MINDSET
FOR THE
NEW GENERATION ORGANISATION

MINDSET

FOR THE
NEW GENERATION ORGANISATION

*How leading SA companies
create counter-trend performance
despite turbulence*

Martin E. Nasser
Frank J. Vivier

1993

JUTA & CO, LTD

ACKNOWLEDGEMENTS

We dedicate this book to those leaders in business and society who so unselfishly shared their insights and experiences regarding the challenges facing the creation of a new generation of organisations — business and government — in Southern Africa. Their contributions have been invaluable.

Our sincere thanks to those participating organisations whose financial contributions made this project possible. We trust that the return on the investment for both the nation and the organisations will be well warranted.

The specialist contributions from the drive tank members: Prof. Leon Brummer, Dr. Azar Jammine, Mr. Don Ncubi, Prof. Lawrence Schlemmer, Dr. Erik Schmikl and Mr. Jerry Schuitema, provided depth and enrichment to this research. In this regard we would also like to thank Prof. Ian MacMillan of the Wharton Graduate School of Business, USA for his particular inputs. Their on-going involvement through months of hard work has been invaluable.

To the core co-ordinating people at Nasser Associates, Mrs. Noekie de Jager and Mrs. Maureen Troy, we say a very special thank you. Their commitment, patience and meticulous dedication were critical to tackling a project of such magnitude. We are indebted to them, their families, and our families for their sacrifices. Last but not least, the efforts and commitment from the executive secretaries of participating organisations have not gone unnoticed. To these many, many talented people we say a very big thank you.

To the hundreds of executives and managers who participated in the interviews and think tanks, our sincerest thanks for adding a qualitative dimension to this study. To the research team headed by Frank Vivier and his very able field research group Derek Ellerbeck, Debbie den Hartog and Gerhard Smit, with much help from many other people, our deepest gratitude. Finally, our thanks to the publishers and the editor.

Amoeba   DISCRETIONARY CREEP

Kop gallop   Cultivated autocrat   ***JUMBO RISKS***

Pup with fleas   COMPETITIVE ANGST

Love bubbles   Rent-a-head-office

ATHLETIC FLEXIBILITY   Submarine syndrome

WHITE HOT   *Corporate chimneys*

Light government   **BEST PRACTICES**

Organisational drag   *STRATEGIC FLING*

Managing through

BIG GORILLA   Value-chain

Strategic schizophrenia   CUSTOMER WORTH

Just-in-time-focus

CONTENTS

The new generation mindset

The common denominator governing the world's leading organisations is the phenomenon of a winning *mindset*. Globally, many of the most significant corporate *turnarounds* have been driven by the power of the leadership mindset. These organisations have progressed from *competitive neglect* and economic decline to large scale renewal. Outstanding examples in recent times are British Airways, General Electric, Boeing, Motorola, Xerox, Honda and such household names in South Africa as First National Bank, Afrox, Southern Sun, Corobrik, Foodcorp, Murray and Roberts, Samcor, Kohler, Randcoal, Sentrachem, Eskom and SA Breweries.

For the majority of South African organisations the future seems less promising. The lack of competitive spirit in South African industry and commerce when the country is poised to re-enter the international arena, is a source of considerable concern to shareholders, analysts and leaders of industry. Increased international competition is forcing a new level of awareness regarding turnaround on a scale never before witnessed in South African business. Jack Schumacher, formerly Vice President of Wallmart — regarded as the world's leading retailer — remarked recently that, while South Africa had all the potential to enter the global arena, the single most important impediment was a mindset among executives which seemed more concerned with maintaining the status quo than dealing with large-scale competition. This is part of the historical South African syndrome and is apparent in the mindset of much of the leadership corps in South Africa — politicians, business people, churchmen and community leaders.

The Project New Generation Economy research indicates that the notion of a winning nation is paramount to South Africa's future, and that the guidelines and processes for developing such mindsets and strategies can be drawn from successful South African organisations.

The nation urgently requires a fundamental shift in the mental framework within which it approaches its destiny. In this regard the lessons learnt from the so-called *counter-trend organisations* can be applied most expeditiously when a fundamentally positive attitude prevails. Many senior business, government and community leaders participating in the research noted that national leaders could, to great advantage, adopt principles emanating from *new generation organisations* in South Africa. While it would be naïve to suggest that South Africa could be managed like a mammoth corporation — South Africa Inc. — it does need to take some *jumbo risks* and reasses the potential of its *invisible assets*. It has been pointed out that both the Latin and Pacific Rim countries' economic revivals and growth have been based on the lessons learnt from successful business practices. They identified *windows of opportunity*, adopted a national winning mindset based on the promise of wealth creation, and above all applied the notion of *light government* to everything they did. In this regard South Africa has more than enough examples of organisations that have survived and grown despite turbulence.

THE IMPACT OF TURBULENCE

The common characteristic of the world economy at present is a high degree of turbulence. Recession has been part of the vocabulary of most Western economies since 1989, and it would appear that there is little chance of a sudden recovery for any of South Africa's traditional trading partners. What is certain, however, from all the information gathered by the research team, is that turbulence will continue unabated, for the forseeable future — albeit in a different format and intensity. Therefore, simple logic indicates that nations and organisations have to be managed for success, in spite of the turbulence. This implies that society's decision-makers must lead from the front in order to generate a *mind shift* which will ensure the best chance of success for the nation. The management of turbulence, therefore, becomes an important new factor in attempting to achieve national success.

The successes achieved in both Asia Pacific and South America in a very short time have focused on the possibility of managing and winning despite such factors as socio-political and socio-economic turbulence. It would seem that while South Africa continues to blame its economic under-performance primarily on the global economic slow-down, the Latin and Pacific Rim countries have used *opportunity-based thinking* as a formula for achieving a *quantum leap* in their economic growth and individual quality of life.

While there has been a substantial amount of work done by a variety of bodies — The National Economic Forum, the Montfleur Initiative, the Old Mutual-Nedcor Studies and Sanlam's "Platform for Growth" initiative, among others — very little has happened to indicate that any significant improvement in the probability of economic prosperity in South Africa is occurring.

Business leaders have noted that the lack of urgent attention being paid to the implementation of an immediate and comprehensive package of recovery strategies in South Africa, is largely due to the apparent paralysis of government and its policymakers. There appear to be several reasons for this impasse:

- The absence of an appropriate common framework for the implementation of such a package among government, business and labour.

- The retardation of effective government responses by the rapid acceleration of political change and the wait for a new government of national unity. There is a sense of paralysis among civil servants who appear to avoid implementing initiatives which could facilitate change, because they fear that such change may be to their detriment.

- The pressing need for a common approach to institutionalising the type of sound management and leadership principles exhibited by new generation nations and organisations by government institutions charged with implementing strategies.

It is imperative that government and business leaders in South Africa overcome the apparent psychological deadlock which prevents them from achieving a national sense of purpose and hope — critical ingredients for a successful economic renaissance.

The present negative psychosis so prevalent in South Africa must be replaced by a focus on the creation of self-destiny. This requires a *framebreaking* approach to envisioning the future and a removal of the fear of failure. The point from which the seeds of enthusiasm, vision and direction-finding grow, originates in the individual and collective national psyche. As this has become such a critical phenomenon the focus of this study is to understand the impact of mindset in redirecting national and organisational destiny.

MINDSET AS THE DETERMINANT OF DESTINY

Mindset is about forging a positive future outcome despite limited opportunities and resources, environmental hostility, socio-economic turmoil and political uncertainty.

Project research has identified the mindset issue as a key determinant of national and organisational destiny. Substantial research and writing since the 60s on the role of the managerial mindset in creating and sustaining organisational health is available. The results are a torrent of literature on diverse topics such as corporate culture, leadership style, executive profiles and a host of managerial processes aimed at giving organisations competitive advantage.

It must, however, be recognised that the concept of mindset on its own, has not been sufficiently emphasised as a determinant of survival and success. It is often viewed as just an outcome of organisational culture or corporate ethos. Project research has identified many examples where the leader's mindset has been the single most important variable in propelling the organisation into an entirely new turn-around position.

To cause an effective and sustainable turnaround in the South African economy, the focus has to be on the development of a psychological stamina as enduring as that of our international competitors'. This stamina will be the most formidable competitive weapon in our national economic armoury.

THE ROLE OF MINDSET IN MANAGING CONDITIONS OF UNCERTAINTY

It is critical that South African leaders develop an appropriate mental framework for coping with large-scale organisational or national turnaround. The key mental block for the leader facing the uncharted waters of large-scale renewal and redirection, is the realisation that there is no fixed blueprint for the future. The outcome of a renewal strategy is uncertain, the prospects of failure are real, and the possibility of collapse due to almost insurmountable problems appears substantial.

The toughest challenge for the leader of turnaround and renewal is to have the courage to step beyond the limits of predictability and the boundaries of conventional paradigms, into unknown terrain. In this domain mindset is a crucial catalyst. One of the prime requirements is the ability to apply lateral thinking, often described as *kop gallop* by South African executives. This provides a *helicopter vision* from which it becomes possible to *leapfrog* previous paradigms.

Recent research has shown that successful turnaround leaders have been good at overcoming the phenomenon called the *event horizon*. The event horizon is that finite line that separates future events — with their uncertain outcomes — from present and past events, where the outcomes are more predictable or known, but often also more sterile. This is the boundary between the visionary forces that create the future, and the forces of limited vision that induce the leader to make decisions that perpetuate the decline of the ailing organisation.

A post mortem of declining organisations and nations shows that ultimate destruction is often precipitated by a series of critical events that have a compounding effect on the psychology of the turnaround leader and his followers. The Rubicon speech of the State President in 1986 is an outstanding example of this. Commercial examples include the demise of the Frame Group, the downward spiral of OK Bazaars — now being reversed by a new CEO — and the initial accumulation of problems at Mossgas. Internationally, the compounding effect of the sequence of events that led to the fall of the chief executive officers at General Motors (Stempel), IBM (Akers), and American Express (Robinson III) are further examples of this phenomenon. Probably the most renowned international example is the Watergate Affair that led to the fall of Richard Nixon.

An analysis of the psychology of such situations shows that each of the events that led to the final watershed is psychologically significant. A correct decision at each critical point would have offered the organisation an opportunity to framebreak out of the downward spiral. When, however, the leader fails to make the required tough decisions, a negative mindset emerges which eventually causes the failure.

A series of "failed events" critically disrupt the forces of gravity that the turnaround leader has created around himself. These forces are used to mould the psyche of his followers into a cohesive vision for the organisation.

The result of such a series of "failed events" is that the event horizon contracts. It becomes increasingly difficult to maintain the mental toughness required to step away from the known and familiar, into the uncertain world beyond.

The growing mental impotence and compounded misjudgements appear to steadily erode the confidence of not only the leader, but the entire leadership core. This increases the *strategic myopia* of the management team. The negative effect is that bolder insights from subordinates are stifled. This creates a deadlock from which it is impossible for the organisation to escape.

In the case of the Rubicon affair and the Watergate scandal, both governments appeared unable to quickly grasp the gravity of the situation, and became politically bankrupt.

In the case of corporate South Africa, where executives do not "grasp the nettle" in time, the net effect is that their chances of survival are increasingly eroded.

Project research has consistently detected this phenomenon in a large number of organisations. The findings suggest that South African leaders need to follow the examples of the counter-trend organisation in order to understand the psychological dynamics facing their organisation and nation.

This book is about understanding the dynamics of this mindset and its application in successful organisations, despite environmental turbulence.

OBJECTIVE OF THE PROJECT

Project New Generation Economy is concerned with investigating the phenomenon of new generation organisations in South Africa, and the application of a new generation of business and management principles for economic revival in the country. The research aims at providing principles, methods and processes for the implementation of new generation mindsets (a prerequisite for economic revival) in South African organisations.

The objective of the project is to identify those generic factors that distinguish counter-trend new generation organisations from traditional-trend organisations.

New generation organisations have developed attitudes, behaviours and practices which have revitalised their ability to create value. In contrast, traditional-trend organisations are characterised by poor economic performance, a lack of competitive stamina, and a mindset that accepts poor performance as part of the wider corporate malaise.

DEFINITIONS

Important building blocks for the research were the definitions of the terms "new generation" and "counter-trend".

- **The concept of "new generation".**

New generation is a term describing those organisations, principles and methods which defy the traditional way of doing things in order to find new horizons for the process of value-creation in organisations in particular, and the nation in general. It implies that the organisation is able to take a quantum leap and effect such major changes as are required to make it a leader in its sector. New generation organisations are recognised for their high degree of innovation, psychological stamina and levels of creative insight.

- **The concept "counter-trend".**

Counter-trend describes new generation organisations which are able to perform despite environmental turbulence — that is, they "buck the trend" of economic performance in the economy. They are typified by their ability to create value despite the many negative factors — including the deteriorating mindset — which surround them. They have a strong belief in their own ability to make things happen. They can overcome their *tunnel vision* and aversion to risk in order to become "can do" organisations.

IDENTIFYING COUNTER-TREND ORGANISATIONS

Counter-trend organisations were identified from data gathered with the assistance of the Bureau of Financial Analysis, University of Pretoria (BFA). All organisations listed on the Johannesburg Stock Exchange were included, augmented by data from stockbrokers, financial analysts, economists and financial press reviews.

Organisations were identified from which suitable data on new generation issues could be obtained. Also included were organisations who had initiated several major interventions which could affect future performance and their ability to adopt new generation thinking. Para-state organisations which were deemed critical to the national wealth-creation potential such as Transnet, the SA Post Office, Eskom, the CSIR, Telkom and the IDC also contributed.

To establish a basis for comparison it was necessary to identify organisations which exhibited below-average levels of economic performance, and where traditional approaches, attitudes, ideas, practices and behaviour prevailed.

From the analysis of all data gathered it became clear that from the identified mindsets, behaviours, attitudes and approaches of counter-trend organisations valuable solutions could be found for ailing organisations and economies.

CHAPTER TWO

Shifting the national mindset

A new paradigm for South African leaders has been uncovered by the research project. It has determined common management principles for managing value creating organisations in South Africa. These principles are generic to both government and business.

Economic revival in South Africa depends on the proficiency of those people who are responsible for the effectiveness of national and corporate performance. In future, all South African leaders will be compelled to emulate the same stringent standards of new generation principles which are inherent in new generation organisations.

While business continues to play a central role in overhauling the economic engine of South Africa, leaders in government, business, the media, labour, communities, churches and politics are being challenged to develop the framework underlying the principles of the new generation nations of the world.

This chapter will address the role of government, the media and business in the creation of a new generation South Africa.

THE ROLE OF GOVERNMENT

Misguided policies in respect of trade and industry, poorly structured market mechanisms, and the ill-conceived execution of economic protection and fiscal policy, have left South Africa in a far worse state in 1993 than it was in ten years ago. Bureaucratic bungling, misappropriation and corruption have compounded the lack of economic growth. As a direct result South Africa has become uncompetitive in terms of world standards. International research on competitive nations highlights the necessity of generating an appropriate economic policy based on a mindset which nurtures and rewards new behaviours which are fundamentally innovative and lead to economic growth. The latest examples of outstanding economic achievements in the short-term are the Latin countries such as Mexico, Chile, Argentina, Columbia and Venezuela, as well as new additions to the Pacific Rim — China, Indonesia, Malaysia, SriLanka, and Vietnam. South Africa is a long way behind these highly energised economic miracles.

Government and business have for too long maintained an adversarial relationship, often extending into metropolitan and regional issues. A *wind tunnel* has developed between these two major players in the economy. Government is viewed as that body which creates regulations and red-tape which tie the hands of business; while business is viewed by government as being concerned only with corporate wealth-creation and the best possible return on assets managed — often at the expense of the larger national picture. These perceptions cause the divergence in the way both parties think. Government is input-driven while business is output-driven. South Africa has much to learn from the way Japan has succeeded in integrating national priorities for business and government to achieve a unified national policy of global intent.

One of the issues fundamental to success is the necessity for government to understand the mechanics and the mindset required to ensure wealth-creation within the global context. Furthermore, government needs to support the same priorities in the interest of creating new horizons for value-adding to the present economy. Capital has been favoured over labour by macro-economic policymakers for far too long. The net effect has been that investment in terms of creating jobs has been inadequate. A focused, visionary industrial and labour policy — referred to in the mid 80s as inward industrialisation — will greatly assist the business and para-statal sectors in developing the total productive capacity of this country. In this regard, the departments of Trade and Industry, Finance, and the SA Reserve Bank have already been grappling with the fundamentals of streamlining economic and industrial policy. This has been strongly supported by the new age approach of the Industrial Development Corporation.

South Africa has a poor track record in terms of the protection of its natural resources, the environment and the social fabric against the excesses of large capital interests. Among South African business leaders there appears to be insufficient balance between capital growth objectives and social and environmental objectives. This issue is becoming one of major international debate. Therefore, it is crucial that macro-economic policy should aim at enforcing a responsible approach to utilising the natural abundance of our country for creating wealth for all South Africans.

THE ROLE OF BUSINESS

Many organisations are suffering from the effects of outdated management approaches, a sense of smugness, uncompetitive organisational designs, impoverished leadership, impotent strategic thinking, dated labour practices and organisational instability. Such impediments as the maintenance of *corporate chimneys*, excessive *clutter*, fixed *decision boundaries*, and dysfunctionality of vertical organisational design have made South African business far less competitive than it would otherwise have been. The extent of *organisational distress* has also been compounded by structural upheaval in our major industries through new entrants, mergers, *competitive shake-out* and *industrial meltdown*. Furthermore, the accelerating international competition — particularly from the Pacific Rim — is expected to create situations requiring turnaround on a scale not witnessed before in South African business.

The incestuousness of South African corporate structures through interlocking shareholder interests is a major impediment to unleashing vast new sources of national wealth-creation. It is a well known fact that 70% of the companies listed on the JSE are controlled by 5 parents. There is an urgent need to enhance the *stakeholder approach* to the governing of the business sector and to dramatically improve the effectiveness of shareholders. Commentators on the inefficiency of South African boards point out the phenomenon of the professional executive director who travels from one board to another, but is seldom able to deliver more than the absolute minimum due to the vast variety of businesses in which he is involved. It is almost impossible to make an effective contribution if a director's attention is spread across an array of diversified business interests. The existence of situations where board directors are attached to boards simply because of their public profiles, is no longer relevant.

The definition of entrepreneurship and *corporate venturing* requires urgent re-appraisal in South Africa. During the 80s and 90s entrepreneurs proved to be key providers of new jobs and new growth for those nations which performed so vigorously in spite of international competition. In this regard we should learn from the very positive experiences of the Latin countries, particularly Mexico, Chile and Argentina. Indications are that the development of entrepreneurship remains an under-developed aspect of our national economy, as a result of government policy on taxation and by-laws towards the providers of capital. The role of the Johannesburg Stock Exchange must not be underestimated with regard to the financial and support base it provides for emerging and established entrepreneurs. In this regard the formation and on-going support for an authentic venture capital market will make a critical contribution to the creation of the thousands of new entrepreneurs so crucial to a new generation economy.

An emerging issue in South Africa is the need for a balance between a company's business growth objectives and the demand for environmentally responsible actions. This is an area that requires considerably more attention to be paid to it than many South African companies are prepared to at present.

THE ROLE OF THE MEDIA

The impact of the media on both opinion leaders and the public in South Africa is well recognized. There has been a proliferation of printed and electronic media over the last ten years. The strength of the impact on individual perceptions at whatever level in society is enormous, and often underestimated.

It is apparent that the media plays a powerful role in setting the national mindset. The research uncovered a firm belief among corporate and government decision-makers that the media was largely responsible for both the confidence index and the fear versus optimism syndromes in society. There has been a propensity for negative reporting in the last five years. The impact on the national consciousness of this continuous negative bombardment has been decidedly destructive. The content and quality of reporting on such issues as politics, violence, company underperformance and corruption has given many business leaders the feeling that, given the present turbulence in South Africa, the future will probably be as uncertain as the present.

An ever-increasing deterioration manifested by poor economic indicators has caused a constant stream of media reporting which emphasises the downward cycle in corporate performance. Business executives are constantly being battered with news of underperforming organisations, poor economic projections and further stagnation. The effect is a feeling of being immersed in a *theatre of the absurd*. Many executives interviewed in this study pinpointed the media as being a major contributor to the sense of economic hopelessness that currently prevails. While negative issues are reported with vigour, positive performance and the thousands of big and small wins tend to be rendered insignificant. The sheer volume of negative reporting has almost overshadowed the miracle performances of many organisations and communities in terms of local and international standards. This study focuses attention on these counter-trend performers and their behaviour. It has become critical that the media begins to pay attention to these very important positive trends in our society in order to act as a positive agent for on-going change.

SUMMARY

In conclusion it must be noted that South Africans, and in particular the opinion leaders, are the architects of our own destiny. In this regard mindset is probably one of the most crucial issues requiring attention. *As we think, so shall we develop.*

CHAPTER THREE

New generation principles

"Great business strategies ... result from a particular state of mind" — Kenichi Ohmae.

Creative insight is the cornerstone of strategic thinking. Organisations that are strong on framebreaking behaviour appear to have an intuitive grasp of the basic elements of strategic thinking. They go beyond the mundane and ordinary, and apply a visionary approach to every aspect of their business.

Probably the most significant finding of the research is that new generation organisations share the common denominators of visionary thinking and a "can do" mindset which appear to account for their ability to perform beyond the ordinary. They are characterised by extraordinary clarity of intent, distinguished by an endless seeking for and seizing of strategic initiative in the markets of their choice. Continuous attention is given to new, creative insights on how to tackle particular issues and processes. It is with this framebreaking mindset as a base that the core issues which distinguish these new generation organisations from their traditional counterparts, are examined.

In discussing the new generation concept it is important to clarify the definition of the success criteria by which organisations are classified as being "new generation".

MEASURING CORPORATE SUCCESS

Gauging outstanding corporate performance often depends on the particular point of view of the researcher. Research by such eminent authorities as Hickman and Pascale shows that neither subjective nor objective tests of company excellence provide a complete yardstick in themselves. South African business observers are more than familiar with the preponderance of financial ratios which are used to dissect corporate performance. Financial performance is often regarded as the single most important factor in judging corporate success. This may be referred to as *singularity of criteria*. The annual ritual performed by such eminent South African publications as *Financial Mail, Finance Week* and *Business Times* in constructing lists of top organisations based on ratios such as asset and equity growth and returns, is well known to most South African executives. A more recent development has been the assessment of superior organisation performance, on the basis of the Market Value-Added (MVA) and Economic Value-Added (EVA) criteria developed by Joel Stern.

While the project team took a great deal of care to evaluate the new generation organisations by means of statistical parameters developed by the Bureau of Financial Analysis at the University of Pretoria, a substantial amount of subjective information was used to augment the initial sample group. The fact that the sample of new generation organisations were at different stages of their life cycles, precluded the use of an exclusive set of criteria and parameters. For example, while a rigid yardstick might be appropriate in assessing mature industries against criteria of market effectiveness and leadership style, it could be quite irrelevant for determining the new generation of potential market leaders in an emerging industry. By adding its own judgement, the research team was able to bring to the study important organisations, which it believed would become major players in a new generation economy.

ORGANISATIONAL LONGEVITY

A key facet of the project was to focus on practices recognised by the respective industries as being essential for long-term sustainable growth and survival. An important key is to avoid the temptation of favouring the short-term, quick-fix approaches, which often appear to be more attractive and less cumbersome than the long-term, more stable solutions. It is imperative that management does not develop *strategic schizophrenia* while attempting to balance short- and long-term objectives. In this study the project team attempted to uncover those factors which focus on organisational longevity, and to avoid those which are essentially transient.

A significant limitation of the data published in recent literature and more popular publications on this matter, is the dependence on the well-tried "secret formula" approach popularised by the landmark work of Peters and Waterman. Recent results indicate that many of the so-called excellent organisations have since disappeared.

Recently, a change has occurred in the thinking of South African managers regarding the idea of committing an organisation to using packaged formulas in an attempt to achieve renewal. These so-called formulas which promised "miracle performance" are now being reviewed with a great deal of scepticism, due to their inability to match expectations.

The 90s appears to be a period in which organisations will become a lot more pragmatic and realistic than they were in the trendy 80s. In the 80s management fads were the order of the day and had a sweeping impact on organisations throughout the country. The dubious, and often negative, reputation of many of the packaged change and renewal strategies has recently prompted many organisations to abandon such programmes in favour of developing indigenous solutions. Using previous experience, a healthy degree of pragmatism, a keen focus on the *tea and coffee issues*, and the assistance of an outside process consultant, organisations have abandoned their addiction to "fad" prescriptions in favour of applying in-house solutions.

CHALLENGES OF STRATEGIC INITIATIVE

New generation organisations are characterised by a strong sense of purpose, rather than merely executing process. In this regard they continually search for insight into three simple, but essential questions:

- How effectively does the organisation engage its markets?
- How effectively does the organisation mobilise its capabilities?
- Does the organisation have the willpower (mental energy) to succeed?

Strategy-making in new generation organisations is driven by a simple, yet dynamic logic that defies conventional, static thinking. According to Ohmae good strategists have a natural talent for thinking idiosyncratically. In this mode the organisation, customers and competitors merge into a dynamic interaction out of which a comprehensive set of objectives and plans, or actions, eventually crystalises, thereby ensuring the extra mile in corporate performance. New generation organisations appear to be blessed with good strategists who have the ability to understand the way in which the market forces, the organisational capability and energy levels among employees need to integrate with each other. These managers are particularly good at providing the necessary *strategic synthesis* which makes for value-added performance. The ability of new generation organisations to view this dynamic interplay from a holistic perspective, enables the organisation to focus attention on pertinent issues. New generation organisations use a series of interlocking questions to develop their strategies and ensure the implementation of such processes as are required for effective renewal of their businesses. Once the strategic intent of the organisation is clear, the challenge is then to mobilise resources which will ensure that the organisation deploys both visible and invisible assets optimally. This puts the organisation firmly in control of its competitive environment. By building upon and directing the organisation's competitive stamina to achieve its long-term objectives, a strategic foothold for growth and financial health is ensured.

TEN NEW GENERATION PRINCIPLES

There are ten key principles which explain the purposeful and directive behaviour of new generation organisations. These are:

- **Engaging the market.** (Discussed in Chapter 4.)
  1. Understand the future.
  2. Create customer value.
  3. Call the tune.
  4. Calculate the risk — then pre-empt.

- **Mobilising capability.** (Discussed in Chapter 5.)
  5. Defy the old paradigms.
  6. Focus on speed, simplicity and self-confidence.
  7. Create an obsession with perpetual renewal.

- **Energising the people.** (Discussed in Chapter 6.)
  8. Nurture competitive angst.
  9. Inspire with pack leadership.
  10. Manage through creative tension.

NEW GENERATION TERMINOLOGY

The research uncovered a rich store of corporate buzzwords that add spice to the debate on the widening gap between emerging new generation organisations and their traditional-trend counterparts. These descriptive terms are used to describe new generation versus traditional-trend concepts, orientation, mindset, behaviour, attitudes, structures and issues. These terms are refreshing, descriptive, amusing and very apt. They are apparently at the core of the newly emerging (but very unofficial) language of new generation organisations.The complete list of these words together with short definitions can be found at the end of the book.

CHAPTER FOUR

Engaging the market

Competitive organisations continue to fascinate researchers because they survive and grow despite turbulence and increasingly complex market challenges.

FOUR KEY PRINICPLES IN ENGAGING THE MARKET

There are four key principles which are critical in the process of engaging the market. These are: understanding the market, creating value for customers, calling the tune, calculating the risk — then pre-empting.

Principle 1: Understand the market

New generation organisations distinguish themselves by grasping the underlying future trends in their markets and their competitive environment. They have a special ability to recognise and proactively seize opportunities, whereas tradtional-trend organisations often merely react in surprise, or continue on their present course in ignorance. This phenomenon is often attributed to the quality of intellectual leadership which new generation organisations seem to posses. There appear to be two requirements for intellectual leadership in an industry:

- A conceptual grasp of the competitive dynamics of the industry. In order to seize the strategic initiative from competitors, managers have to recognise the driving forces that shape the future of the industry and grasp the future possibilities that may arise from the interplay between these forces. This leadership is often able to grasp new notions and identify opportunities e.g. *white hot* industries.

- A quick identification of these opportunities for exploiting future possibilities, and the preparedness to timeously build the future competitive capability of the organisation (eg. competence, resources, assets). This leadership is particularly good at understanding where and when the *rubber hits the road*.

The essence of intellectual leadership in an industry is captured by the following scenario: Imagine that your management team is invited to a gathering of the top 100 people in your industry. During the proceedings each participant is required to list those individuals whom they secretly admire for their understanding of the forces that govern the future of their industry. Furthermore, these people must be viewed as opinion leaders in the industry and their organisations must be regarded as trendsetters in the economy. When the results of the final short list are announced, how many members of your own management team would appear among the top five names? If your organisation has a substantial number of such individuals, then there is obviously no problem. If, on the other hand, there are few or no individuals on this list, the question then is for how long is your organisation likely to survive, given that the intellectual leaders in the industry set the pace and keep changing the rules for others like yourself to follow? How long will it be before your organisation becomes obsolete?

An interesting example of an organisation that has emerged from the realm of para-statal existence towards commercialisation, is the Rotek group. The organisation has distinguished itself among its peers by seizing the moment, identifying future trends, grasping opportunities and being bold enough to face up to them.

Rotek was created from what was the central maintenance service of Eskom in 1988 when the total operation was placed on a commercial footing. It consists of expertise and facilities in the fields of mechanical and electrical engineering, heavy transport and vehicle refurbishment, civil engineering, property management and other related activities. Since then Rotek has established itself as a force in its respective market, rising from a position of substantial loss and uncertain market prospects.

Under the visionary leadership of the CEO, Bruno Penzhorn, Rotek has achieved a considerable turnaround using bold strategies, inspirational leadership and an ability to capitalise on future trends. Penzhorn and his executive have been particularly successful in understanding how to capitalise on future market needs in their respective business areas, and moulding the once unfocused and bureaucratic organisation into a leaner, more agressive business that is prepared to tackle the competition on equal terms. An example of the group's futuristic thinking is their willingness to create an organisation that can become a role model for industrial relations in a future South Africa. Recently, the group activated a bold approach to revolutionise their long-term industrial relations policy in view of the transformation in South Africa. When the organisation identified the impact of recent international developments on the thinking of key role players such as COSATU, NUMSA and SEIFSA, the organisation moved swiftly to gain firsthand insight into these international developments. One of these developments is the Australian Model which has aparantly had a key influence on the thinking of organised labour such as NUMSA. Rotek wished to ensure that their policies were aligned with such international trends.

Interestingly, SA has much to gain from the Australian Model. A critical feature of the model is its holistic approach to identifying national objectives for the achievement of internationally recognised levels of economic and competitive performance. These objectives have been consolidated at the national level in an integrated *benchmarking* and *best practices* policy guideline. In this regard Rotek has aimed at a policy of benchmarking itself against the trendsetters in industrial relations development and training. For an organisation that faced such a steep learning curve in free market competition, it shows surprising levels of insight into the challenges facing the new South Africa.

Another recent relevant example of a para-statal organisation that has moved into the commercial mode at a very rapid rate is the SABC. The national broadcaster — despite all the political turmoil surrounding it in the recent appointment of its new board — is gearing itself to becoming a world class player. The SABC is attempting to uplift the quality of its programming standards to equal those of the world's best broadcasters. Furthermore, it is paying substantial attention to selling its programmes into the international market. It has understood that the future is about global communication, and that to enter the world arena the product has to be exceptional.

A major example of a conglomerate that successfully grapples with the issue of the future is the Murray & Roberts group. In the past five years, under the very able leadership of David Brink, the group has repositioned itself, not only in terms of its core businesses, but also its management processes. From being a highly centralised organisation, it has moved towards independent, autonomous business units in which real empowerment has been instituted throughout the system by a flattening of the structure and the creation of *deep jobs* within the group. The chief executive has been singular in disallowing the protection of holy cows inherited from the past. The organisation has invested a great deal of time and money in understanding and involving its people and their communities in all facets of the business. The M&R group has become well known for its dual-logic approach to managing its businesses. For the high technology state-of-the-art global businesses within the group the approach is one of becoming capital intensive in an effort to compete with the best in the world. In terms of the group's local and African businesses, the focus is on a developing world approach in which labour intensiveness is emphasised at the cost of technology intensiveness. Management in M&R understands that the future involves competing globally and also creating jobs locally. This is in keeping with the kind of future that they have anticipated for South Africa until the year 2000. In continuing to emphasise this focus management has understood that there would have to be an on-going *re-engineering* of the business, as and when the circumstances demand it.

A prime example of an organisation which has seized its destiny by understanding the future is M-Net. By seizing on the vast untapped demand for quality television it has captivated South Africans with a diet of international class entertainment. Unlike its major competitor it has steered away from traditional news making, and has focused on fulfilling the entire family's needs — escapism, education and leisure. In the process it has mastered the art of segmentation.

Recognising the emerging opportunities for international electronic media networks, M-Net took the bold step of purchasing the European pay TV Group, Filmnet in a consortium with Richemont. In the process M-Net has focused on building strategic alliances with international organisations in order to ensure rapid global entry. It is currently revamping the entire structure, nature and focus of its business in the belief that the magic M-Net formula will captivate the European consumers' imagination in much the same way as it did in South Africa. It is bringing hype to what was previously a somewhat dull 24 hour movie channel in Europe and Scandinavia.

Principle 2: Create value for the customer

The objective of the entire new generation organisation is to be obsessed with creating value for the customer. New generation organisations have discovered that the only source of competitive advantage is an all-consuming drive to create customer value, and eradicate value-limiting activities — everything else is peripheral detail. In contrast, their traditional-trend counterparts are fixated on the conventional approach of competitor advantages.

Traditional-trenders follow a conventional approach with strategies aimed at increasing the perceived benefits of their products and services. New generation organisations, however, emphasise the need to maintain a balance between strategies which are intended to create value, and those which aim at eradicating activities, processes, procedures, policies and attitudes that kill customer perceptions of value.

The advantage of the latter approach is that while benefit-building strategies typically require capital outlays (e.g. technology to increase product functionality) strategies which aim at eliminating value-reducing activities primarily require a shift towards an *initiative-seeking culture* in which everybody plays a role. The culture in new generation organisations is one in which people are expected to have two jobs in parallel:

- to perform those tasks required of the job;
- to remove those activities that kill customer perception of value.

Issues that kill customer value have become known as the *nothingness* in the workflow value-chain. The approach is highlighted by the philosophy of Jan Carlson, CEO of SAS. He believes that it is both immoral and illegal for an organisation to allow people to perform activities for which the customer has to pay, but which are not perceived as having any additional value for the customer. It would therefore seem logical that creating customer value should be the major context within which businesses operate. There are, however, two significant mental impediments to the attempt by large traditional organisations to establish this simple concept as their main point of departure:

- The extent to which self-centered head office support functions are allowed to dominate the organisational agenda with non-critical, non-operational issues. This causes a distortion of the integrity of the strategic value-chains in the business. Whereas line operations should determine the priorities and service levels of support functions, support functions in traditional-trend organisations have instead become a law unto themselves.

They have become order givers, instead of order supporters.

- The extent to which traditional-trend organisations, while implementing renewal processes, fail to recognise that an organisation cannot be "half pregnant". For example, half measures cannot be taken in collapsing the vertically structured functions in favour of a horizontal structure of value-chains (cross-functional workflow). The organisation has to go all the way if it is serious about the changes.

Project research identified a number of organisations that have confronted these issues head-on. Corobrik is an organisation that required extraordinary effort to illuminate the mental black hole that threatened the decay of its ability to create customer value. The performance of this organisation, once the dominant giant in the clay brick market in South Africa, has in recent years been sliding fairly dramatically. The negative growth which pervaded the organisation by 1989 is typical of many of South Africa's first-world industry leaders.

Since the 70s increasing complacency and creeping bureaucracy, exacerbated by a myopic investment approach from the shareholder, have taken their toll of Corobrik. With prices escalating, after-sales service diminishing and product quality remaining the same, customer loyalty moved from Corobrik to a host of other producers including cement brick manufacturers. The challenges of a rapidly changing market were not sufficiently understood or coped with by the organisation. To add to its problems the following issues were also identified:

- Production concerns rather than market requirements dominated product development;
- Technology had become outdated;
- Plant re-engineering requirements were met by freezing most non-mandatory capital projects; and
- Productivity was continuously declining.

Figure 1. Identifying the Competitive Gap

In addition, the organisation was losing its grip on the market through poorly formulated counter-responses to the arrival of a wide range of small and medium-sized competitors who were changing the very face of the brick industry in South Africa. The most evident sign of Corobrik's competitive neglect was the mindset exhibited by management. With hindsight it is obvious that the challenge of turning the mindset of an established, but fallen industry leader from a position of lethargy and insecurity, to one of resilience and competitive stamina, required a great deal more effort than management estimated. In addition a high degree of *corporate malaise* was evident within Corobrik. The deterioration of the construction sector did nothing to alleviate the pain of this once formidable giant. Under these circumstances management woke up with a bang. With the determined guidance of Errol Rutherford, Group Executive Chairman, the organisation came to recognise that the only issue of importance was that of regaining its ability to create value for its customers at prices they could afford. The issue was to understand the competitive gap (see Figure 1).

Several years of rationalisation, restructuring, culling back on production capacity and decreasing non-essential expenditure, had not delivered the anticipated benefits. Bold, new direction was urgently required. The concept of managing the *customer encounter* was introduced into the business as a mainstream process. The approach used by Corobrik in creating total customer value for money was no different from that used by Ampros, Standard Engineering, Avis, Santam and Telkom — all striving to create new perceptions in the customers' mind about superior worth for the consumer rand.

Ampros's Gerald Leisner, Avis' Glen van Heerden, Santam's Jannie Geldenhuys, Standard Engineering's Hugh Brown, and Jet Stores' Don Etheridge, like Rutherford, forcefully challenged their managements to question their long-held assumptions about the factors that had ensured their organisation's traditional competitive advantages. They all adopted a very strong approach towards the customer —

became customer obsessed — in order to re-establish a positive perception among their customers regarding worth. All these very successful executives recognised the strong need for inspirational leadership in creating a paradigm shift to establish customer obsession.Their managements recognised that in order to become or remain a *leading-edge business*, they had to nuture the ability to learn quicker and respond faster than the rest of the industry.

Rutherford, like all his successful counterparts led a direct attack on issues that destroyed customer value. He instituted an organisational renewal process aimed at eradicating work, structures, processes and activities that failed to create customer value. By calling *Town Hall meetings* and using a structured process, employees, customers and suppliers were brought together face-to-face for the first time in many years. The focus was on instilling a common vision for creating superior customer value.

The mindset developed in Corobrik, Ampros, Avis, Santam and Jet Stores was that of revolutionising the customer encounter in their respective industries. In the case of Corobrik, 18 months after the introduction of the renewal process and the new philosophy, the first fruits were borne. The organisation began to regain its lost local market share, while a radically new approach to providing a total package of benefits (instead of merely setting a pricing policy) clearly signalled the re-entry of Corobrik as a hungry and focused competitor. To add to the excitement, after several additional months of tireless effort, the organisation gained a substantial export order for face bricks to Singapore. This was achieved despite strong international competition, including Australian producers, who had a considerable advantage in terms of distance and transportation cost. This export order had the immediate, desired effect of galvanising the various operations in the group into a level of frenetic activity in order to ensure that the stringent standards of reliability, quality and delivery could be achieved on the export order. This initial breakthrough has now become legendary and its impact on the organisation has been phenomenal. This increasing self-confidence and attention to detail has enabled Corobrik to gain further new markets in the highly competitive international arena. In fact, indications are that Corobrik has suddenly surged ahead as the largest exporter of face bricks internationally.

In all these organisations there has been a strong rejuvenation, and the framebreaking thinking that formed the basis of the managements' mindset has cascaded throughout the rest of the organisation. The most important factor contributing to this success has been that management has become totally visible in practicing the framebreaking thinking needed for creating a new approach to customer interest.

An organisation noted for its intense focus on the customer is SA Breweries. When Group Chairman Myer Kahn was asked to identify the key focus point over the next ten years, he simply commented: "I can't see that anything has changed. The business starts with a product. At the end of the road consumer goods businesses are like politicians. We have an election every day of our lives. Our consumers vote with their throats. We count the cash. Everything starts and finishes with the product". Chief Executive of the Group, Graham Mackay echoes these sentiments with even greater enthusiasm. He believes that the customer is the ultimate king and that everything that is done in Beer Division should be built around customer needs and preferences.

Mackay is acutely aware of the danger of a market leader becoming complacent. He is always aware of the possibility of corporate malaise creeping in among his executives. In this regard his concern is no different from that of FNB's Barry Swart, Foschini's Clive Hirschsohn, Afcol's Tom Eccles and Keith Roger-Lund, and SAA's Mike Myburgh. Their attention is aimed at ensuring a constant level of *creative tension* within their organisations. This is focused on providing superior customer value for money. Quality and affordability are key factors to which constant attention is paid by every employee. SAB Beer Division in particular, emphasizes the need to create *continuous discontent* with existing levels of customer service.

The CSIR is yet another excellent example of an organisation which has made considerable progress in creating value for the customer. Emerging from the comfort of being totally government-sponsored, and having no history of profit accountability, the organisation has had to move into top gear in order to deal with head-on local and international competition, and generate profits in the process.

The notion of creating customer value as the fundamental *raisson d'etre* of the organisation was the idea of Dr Brian Clarke and his executive at the CSIR. For them the strategy was to find a one-stop research, technology development and transfer service for most of South Africa's needs. Be these from the large, medium and small enterprises or micro-enterprises in the informal sector; society at large, especially urban and rural developing communities; or from policy-makers in government and the private sector. The notion of serving as a technology partner was born out of a desire to create a service which was unparallelled in this country. Turning a scientific organisation which was prescriptive into one which is customer driven has not been an easy task. Through its strategies, education and development programmes however, management has changed the mindset of its employees from being endless absorbers of capital for scientific research to being output-driven — able to deliver a return on investment for the capital invested in research.

The move away from being input-driven to becoming an output focused organisation has also been reflected in the major strides made in Eskom, Transnet, Portnet and Spoornet. In adapting themselves to meeting the challenge of creating customer value, they have had to restructure their entire organisations and refurbish their managerial mindsets. In many cases these organisations have developed *skunk works* in an effort to move from a slog mode to one of slipstreaming past obstacles towards new-found opportunities.

It has required the calibre of Transnet's Dr Anton Moolman, Eskom's Dr Ian McRae, and their various chief executives to cause the major mindshifts required over a relatively short period of time. These organisations are in the midst of an extensive overhaul towards becoming customer obsessed.

Typically, structures have had to be altered from a steep pyramid towards a flattened format. Size has been considerably reduced from *corporate obesity* to an *athletically flexible* system. This is reflected in the increased levels of accountability and responsibility, elimination of *upward creep*, initiation of a culture of urgency and cost awareness, and the divestment of businesses which did not fit the future vision of the organisations. These non-fit businesses are identified as *pups with fleas*.

One of the dominant retail fashion and accessory businesses in the South African market is Edgars Stores. During the last ten years in particular the Group has re-aligned itself and through its businesses, Edgars, Jet Stores, Sales House and Celrose, it has concentrated on a number of specialised market niches. The optimum focus of all these businesses has been the emphasis on quality at an affordable price, augmented by an extensive credit network. Using its highly professional buying departments, manufacturing units, distribution chains and its quality control functions, the business has established a leading value-for-money image for itself in South Africa.

Principle 3: Call the tune

Research has shown that the successful strategist continuously seeks opportunities for upsetting the industry equilibrium. According to Prof. Ian MacMillan (Wharton Graduate School of Business), this implies pursuing strategies that will allow the organisation to disrupt the normal course of industry events and create new industry conditions to the disadvantage of competitors.

Jack Welch (CEO of GE) one of the world's most formidable business strategists, explained his efforts to regain the key strategic foothold in each of General Electric's markets by thinking as follows: "To be content to be third or fourth position in your industry is foolish. One morning you will wake up and find that number one or two has changed the rules of the game. What use is all your effort then. You may very well find that you have slid from being third or fourth, to sixth or seventh".

Dominance is a key issue which cannot be ignored. It is introduced in all counter-trend organisations as a *corporate ideology*. It is a core strategy in the armoury of many of South Africa's leading-edge organisations. For instance, M-Net and its various overseas subsidiaries have become well known for their ability to upstage the broadcasting industry's thinking. M-Net has broken conventional paradigms in establishing itself as a leading pay TV broadcaster in Africa. Its newly acquired overseas pay TV business Filmnet, is aiming to achieve the same objective of dominance, albeit in very tough circumstances. From humble beginnings in the face of almost insurmountable regulatory restrictions M-Net has done exeptionally well for all its stakeholders.

A distinguishing characteristic of M-Net is its opportunistic flair, aggressiveness and long-term strategic frame of reference, which greatly assist in defying the logic of the industry and M-Net's competitors. The Chief Executive, Koos Bekker has been attributed with having a very competitive mindset. Industry insiders suggest that Bekker had already developed his global vision prior to the formal establishment of his South African business roots.

The particular strength of the M-Net executive team has been its uncanny ability to upstage the established TV media from the start. This is primarily a result of its formidable ability to keep competitors off-balance with a string of unsuspected moves and counter-moves aimed at changing industry rules, or at least checking competitor developments.

The astounding pace with which M-Net is able to seize opportunities, establish the required *core competencies* and then *leapfrog* into new markets, is unequalled in the local industry. A good example is the speed at which M-Net recently introduced international channels such as the BBC to their menu of subscriber channels in South Africa and Africa. This caught the industry totally unprepared.

The characteristics of speed and action are not unique to M-Net. In organisations such as Ellerines, ISG, Mondi Paper Company, Metropolitan Life and Sasol, the emphasis is on pro-activeness in understanding the market and then acting with athletic flexibility to ensure that the available opportunities are capitalised on in the fastest possible time. Each of these organisations have become acutely aware of the *big gorilla* in their particular sectors, and are constantly striving to be smarter than this dominant animal.

Ellerines has always outpaced its major rivals in establishing new sites, carrying new furniture and appliance ranges and developing entirely new sales and credit processes for driving its business in the black consumer market. This has created the rules for rivals to follow. Similarly ISG, Metropolitan Life and Sasol have called the tune in terms of their specific industries. Metropolitan Life for instance, has created the rules of the game for insurers in the black consumer market. Sasol on the other hand, has been a trendsetter in the chemicals industry, not only locally but also internationally, and has been instrumental in shifting both the focus and initiatives in the chemical sector. This has often been strongly censured by its major rivals who believe that Sasol has had an unfair advantage in using state-acquired assets cheaply, to the detriment of the industry.

M-Net considers dominant core competencies and sustainability to be vital prerequisites for long-term initiative. In order to achieve this the organisation has created new rules by developing a range of additional services attached to its existing portfolio of products and services, thus capitalising on its existing subscriber base. Industry observers suggest that M-Net is poised to become a pioneer in creating television users from its present base of television viewers through new age "technology-from-home" services. Note, for instance, its bid to lead the emerging cellular telephone industry in combination with interactive multi-media television services. In support of these developments the organisation has already entrenched itself as a leader in customer service ethics amongst its peers in the entertainment and services industries.

A major danger facing all high-growth organisations is the loss of their ability to act like small, entrepreneurial businesses which have the benefits of speed and simplicity while also enjoying the advantages of size and the resources of a large organisation. They fear that by tightening up their organisations they could develop *corporate anorexia* which would leave them severely impeded, particularly in times when they need the extra stamina required to deal with the intrusions of the big gorilla.

Engen, the most recent addition to the Gencor stable, is a conglomerate consisting of the original Mobil refinery and Trek, Sonap and Mobil distribution and marketing organisations. Since inception, the Chief Executive Rob Angel, has emphasised a never-ending pursuit of dominance as the major producer, refiner and supplier of petroleum products in the Southern African market. In addition new horizons have emerged for the expansion of Engen into a number of international locations, including Asia Pacific, Africa and South America. In order to become and remain a dominant force in the world energy market it has been necessary to adjust the fundamental structures and processes of the entire organisation. For the Engen executive the key issue is to be recognised and perform as a major competitive force and to dominate those niches in the market which it has identified as being in the best interests of its various stakeholders. From a big, cumbersome, slow-moving petroleum business, it is moving towards a tightly-knit, market responsive organisation which can respond with alacrity to the opportunities available in the marketplace.

The most successful food retailer in South Africa is unquestionably Pick 'n Pay. From its humble beginnings some 25 years ago, Chief Executive Raymond Ackerman caused chaos in the marketplace by changing all the rules of the game in the retail sector. On issues such as customer service, pricing, merchandising, supplier relationships, and a vanguard for the consumer, Mr Ackerman has become an un-paralleled champion, who has forced every participant in the industry to review their efficiencies and processes in their interface with the consumer. He has pioneered many new concepts in the retailing domain and competitors have been forced to follow suit. The competitors, therefore, can never be complacent for too long. Pick 'n Pay is today a household name in food retailing and is regarded as being synonomous with value-for-money and an important agent for change.

Telkor, under the leadership of its Chief Executive Dave King, has become a significant force in the local and international telephone supply market. In the short space of five years, it has moved from being an insignificant supplier of pay telephones to a dominant force in this and other markets. Determined to become a number one player, it has invested a great deal of R&D to penetrate both local and international markets. The corporate ethos which Dave King has established is that the South African manufacturer must be able to compete with the best in the world. In this case that meant Swiss, German and Japanese competition. Through its continuous striving for dominance, it became a world leader in developing coin validation systems which have enabled the organisation to penetrate world markets and dominate the East European pay telephone market.

More important is the newly-acquired technology that has helped to change the ground rules for pay telephone companies around the world. These achievements have been made possible by stressing creativity in every single function within the business, and gearing Telkom's management process towards value-adding to the existing technology and markets. The *corporate canvas* which Dave King and his management have painted reflects the high degree of creativity and value-adding inherent in this managements' mindset. Telkor's achievement is remarkable by any standard, particularly when one recognises that it is pitted against such world giants as Phillips, Siemens and AT & T.

Santam has become very well known for its multiplex umbrella in the short-term insurance industry. From a reasonably introverted Cape based organisation some 15 years ago, it has developed into a highly confident dominator in the short-term insurance market. With a constant stream of new initiatives and a farsighted product range, the organisation has called the tune and changed the ground rules in becoming the industry leader on short-term insurance in this country. The prime requirements for achieving this have been the innovation at executive level, as well as flexibility and rapid response-time of the entire organisation.

An example of a professional services firm that has changed the rules in its industry, is the century-old Johannesburg based legal firm, Bell, Dewar & Hall. Legal firms have been notorious for their country-club approach to managing their business affairs, while remaining exclusive, smug and content about their enduring livelihood. Under the bold leadership of Andrew Mitchell, the managing partner, the firm recently refurbished its strategic intent by completely redefining its market focus. The breakthrough was the result of shifting its focus from "waiting for the client" approach towards the "managing our clients' legal risks" way of doing business. This shift in emphasis ensured the eradication of the old paradigms about the way the firm conducted its business. Pro-activeness, innovation, flexibility and optimisation of resources have since become the hallmarks of the firm. It has achieved impressive earning ratio levels in the legal sector with productivity, in terms of average fees earned per employee, being impressive by any standard.

Principle 4: Calculate the risk — then pre-empt

Creative insight and boldness change the direction of the business and the rules of the game. New generation organisations often exhibit flair and willpower in executing uniquely conceived strategies which defy the laws of orthodoxy. Often they surprise industry observers by moving the focus of their organisations from one direction to another in the face of traditional wisdom— after having calculated the opportunity of an open window. In such organisations where creative insight is used as a direction finder, the chemistry is one of continuous discontent, *continuous stretch*, continuous improvement and an on-going search for new opportunities. Organisations such as Dorbyl, Kohler, Sanlam, RandCoal, Plessey, SA Druggists, Spescom and Sentrachem have had success in pre-empting market trends by taking the necessary calculated risks in opening new horizons for their organisations.

One of the best known, recent examples of the creative approach to entrepreneurial thinking, is the newly formed McCarthy Retail Group (merger of McCarthy & Prefcor). Their pre-emptive strategies have changed the source of competitive advantage by shifting the industry's goalposts. While the approach of the Group has its fair share of sceptics, it has certainly caused raised eyebrows and considerable interest among competitors, analysts and observers.

Prefcor has shown enormous ingenuity in identifying unconventional business opportunities and capitalising on them. One example was its increasing concern about the size of its debtor book. Realising that managing large debtor accounts was not its forte, and that it would be in the business's best interests to lessen the strains that this placed on the resources of the business, Prefcor created First Pref in alliance with First National Bank. This provided a new business opportunity for Prefcor whose predicament was a common feature of the clothing and furniture industry.

More recently the merger between Prefcor and McCarthy into a major diversified retailing group saw another outstanding, albeit unorthodox and controversial, application of the same principle. Under the leadership of Terry Rosenberg this organisation spread itself across a portfolio covering the retailing and servicing of motor vehicles to the retailing and servicing of appliances and big ticket items. Although these may seem highly diversified businesses, the application of the principles remains identical.

Many competitors have described this strategy as being dysfunctional. Terry Rosenberg, however, saw this move as one which was counter-trend by dumping the *cultural baggage* of past strategic conventions in favour of taking the kind of risks which were necessary in a rapidly changing marketplace. The key behind McCarthy Retail's innovative approach is the realisation that the bulk of the core business is generated by existing customers who have long-standing goodwill towards the Group and whose personal details (demographics, credit record, family profile, income) were known to the organisation, due to the fact that the large majority used credit provided by the group. Thus it would make sense to capitalise on the core customer base by attaching extended products and services to the existing menu. The Group decided on a bold strategy to capture the more than 1 million existing customers through additional products such as financial purchasing arrangements. Most of the customer base had seldom been offered access to credit or insurance by the existing institutions, due to the perceived high risk profile — a result of bad debt projections and township violence. Therefore McCarthy Retail moved with speed to pre-empt more conventional competitors, and according to the latest indications, have already attracted sufficient business to cover the initial capital outlay.

Eskom, the largest supplier of electricity in Southern Africa, has moved away from being a giant state-subsidised organisation, towards being a focused business in the domain of energy needs. Probably its most significant recent action has been its entry into the supply of electricity for third world and rural populations.

By drastically altering its technology, cost structure, pricing policy and process of electrical distribution, it has developed an entirely new market for over 3 million consumers of electric power. In achieving this it had to cut across all traditional decision boundaries which were part of the original tunnel vision so characteristic of the Eskom risk profile. While the risk was high, it has proved to be a smart, calculated move to capture the imagination of a large component of third world people by providing access to the benefits of domestic electricity.

A particular forte Eskom has developed in recent years, is the ability to create lasting relationships with the communities they supply. The Group has achieved considerable progress through revolutionising their image as an important role-player in constructing a stable, healthy, and growth oriented community life. An important contributor to their hard-won credibility among community leaders, local government bodies, socio-political groups and organised labour is the extent to which Eskom is becoming a role model for organisational democracy. Devolution of decision-making and empowerment of all stakeholders, including employees, has made it possible for this democracy to come alive. Under the bold leadership of their CEO Ian McRae, Eskom has decided to embark on a risky new strategy to transform their organisational fabric by ensuring a level playing field for all stakeholders. For instance, union leaders are forming an important component part of the strategic decision-making processes of the business. Recent indications are that union views contributed in selecting the new CEO, Alan Morgan. It is also expected that union views will be represented on the new Eskom council.

More recently Eskom has been making substantial pre-emptive investments to find other innovative applications for electricity, either live or "stored". One such example is the investment currently being made in the development and distribution of electric motor vehicles. This is already meeting with considerable success. All these achievements were not possible without major mindshifts throughout the organisation — particularly at the executive level, from where these new thrusts emerged.

Transnet, in adopting the commercial mantle, was forced into a new position of calculated risk. Whereas before it had been entirely input-driven, the focus now was on an output measured organisation moving away from a centralised, unfocused entity towards a business which consisted of 19 different SBU's. Deregulation in South Africa has made it possible for air, road and sea transportation to be opened to a host of new competitors — previously barred from entering this market. The risks were not only financial, but involved such decisions as selling off what had previously been core businesses, *outsourcing* much of what had previously been in-house activities, and re-designing the entire organisation and management roles within the various businesses. Transnet had to apply the principle of *light government* and *interlocking partnerships* — both new risk areas for the organisation — in moving towards its new focus. A dramatic learning curve was required to attain its new vision of commercialisation.

From being state dependent the CEO, Dr Anton Moolman, has moved this organisation to a position of financial self-sufficiency. Today, with its 135 000 employees throughout its various businesses, the company is substantially different from the position it was in during 1985 when over 279 000 people where part of SA Transport Services. Productivity is up, costs are down, and the organisation has started to develop a reputation for its business-like approach.

One of the major examples of pre-empting with calculated risk is the SBDC. In its mission to search for, develop and nurture small business in South Africa this organisation has done a remarkable job of using risk for the purpose of creating new ventures. The able leadership of Dr Ben Vosloo has made it possible for the SBDC to become a major development agency in encouraging the entrepreneurial mindset in South Africa.

It is important to note that the emphasis is on calculated risk and that a great deal of hard research is conducted on each proposal before it reaches the professional officers who make the lending decisions on new ventures. The results speak for themselves. Dr Vosloo claims that the cost per job generated via the SBDC formula, is the lowest in South Africa — R3 000 per new job.

An interesting new entrant to the commercial arena is the SA Post Office. This was previously a state-owned corporation but has become an organisation which is entirely focused on self-sufficiency. Whereas the organisation had been almost entirely inward focused, the emphasis now is on a mind switch towards understanding the marketplace and the notion of profitability. The tunnel vision has been replaced with a helicopter vision, which is concerned with value-creation in its approach to the marketplace. In looking for new solutions to running the SA Post Office, such options as franchising the sale of postal stamps, services and products have taken a total paradigm shift. It is now a well-known fact that the retailing industry in this country is becoming a major distributor of the SA Post Office's products. This framebreaking approach to selling its products has caused a great deal of attention in corporate South Africa. No-one ever imagined that this could be possible. But CEO Hennie Diedericks, together with his senior management, was determined to follow world patterns in this regard and follow them he did — with all the risks commensurate with such a decision.

A final example of what can be done to make entrepreneurs out of comfortable organisations is the experience of the city of Durban. The city was, until 1985, typically managed by bureaucrats and led by elected politicians. It then broke away from the traditional government role and followed the notion of running the city like a business organisation. The calculated risk was in moving away from the traditional input focused model towards one in which the future of local government was judged by its ability to deliver relevant outputs for all its stakeholders. The management process was entirely re-designed and the whole approach to city financing moved away from a cost plus inflation approach towards improving efficiency and value-creation for the stakeholder. In taking these risks the city moved away from its traditional toe-dipping approach towards new wave thinking in restructuring its financing and managerial processes. The results led to a new level of cost conciousness and a constant questioning of the value-adding being achieved by the different divisions within the Council.

A brand new approach to financial investment was also adopted and this led to highly innovative schemes for investing funds and capital to develop metropolitan infrastructure. The result is that Durban is today the most financially self-sufficient city in South Africa with its annual increases in rates and taxes being under the inflation index.

A further example of local government taking on a brand new pre-emptive mantle is that of the City Council of Pretoria. The Council has turned its attention away from being a control-oriented bureaucracy towards being a new user-friendly "partner". In its quest to encourage entrepreneurial and capital investment the Council has taken giant steps in transforming the by-laws on a host of issues governing development. It has gone out of its way to woo foreign investors by, for example, sending a trade delegation to the Far East. Furthermore, by appointing a Director of Marketing it has launched a strong commercial initiative for Pretoria.

In terms of the new South Africa Pretoria is attempting to create a climate of harmony, cooperation and economic prosperity for all its citizens. It has been proactive in promoting all the elements of change needed to ensure a "smoother" transition to the new format of local government in South Africa.

KEY CONSIDERATIONS IN ENGAGING THE MARKET

Project research has identified a number of key issues facing organisations in their attempts to optimally engage present markets and find new investment opportunities.

Mental metamorphosis

South African management has come under increasingly sharp criticism for allowing a lack of competitiveness to erode their market positions. Debate has been conducted about the need for a mental metamorphosis, in order to remove the deeply rooted paradigm that managers cannot be held fully accountable for their corporate performance due to the adverse external factors. It therefore becomes critical to analyse the question of ensuring *self-destiny* during times of adversity.

New generation organisations recognise that the main task of management is to cope with the demands made by internal forces of change, such as organisational structure, culture, business synergy, core competencies and renewal. This often demands a new *lightness on the feet* approach, particularly when environmental changes compel the organisation to dismantle present strategies and cost structures at a rapid pace and replace these with enduring recovery strategies.

Moreover, project research in counter-trend organisations found that these organisations, irrespective of the nature, size and location of the business, believed that management remains solely responsible for the organisation's ability to cope with the shifts in the external environment. They all strongly emphasise the notion of taking charge of one's own destiny. In fact, the ability of new generation organisations to guide their decision-makers away from obsolete historical strategic assumptions toward a new set of strategic imperatives in a very short space of time, is quite remarkable.

In contrast, traditional-trend organisations flatly refuse to accept responsibility for their organisations' inability to function optimally in a severely disrupted market situation. Managers in these organisations did not hesitate to point out that turbulence in the environment was the prime reason for poor business performance and that they could not be held accountable for these.

No wonder that traditional-trend organisations are notoriously poor in getting decision-makers to accept responsibility for business variables. The question: "What are the enduring elements in this business that will allow us to *trade our way out of the corner*, and what are the issues we should deal with?" generally causes enormous debate. It highlights the inability to seize control of one's destiny by accepting responsibility for all the management variables.

Learning to adapt to the market

A major task for the CEO is to ensure that his management team is able to adjust its paradigms as rapidly as the environment changes. In this regard the ability to accurately assess the market signals is of vital importance.

There are a number of techniques being used by many organisations to assist managers to understand the new signals in the market environment and to respond appropriately. Project research has identified several traditional-trend organisations which prefer elaborate planning cycles, sophisticated scenarios, brain-storming sessions and extensive market research to understand their competitive environments. A pre-requisite for such an approach is the need for a keen intellectual capability on the part of managers. Furthermore, these organisations have developed their approach over many years by tried and tested methods in order to evolve their own planning system.

An important new development is the extent to which new generation organisations have simplified and improved their conventional approach to reading new signals from the market. The new approach is distinguished by a more sensible use of scientific market research.

For instance, there is a shift away from using market research findings as the major anchor for corporate planning. New generation organisations concentrate comparatively less effort on market research information and more on a gut feel and understanding of their markets. For them the key issues are the pull factor — customer demand — and the push factor — market forecasts. These are used in the design, production, sale and servicing of their products. In these organisations management is continuously challenged to vigorously debate the findings of their research department. Skunk works are often used as the process for ensuring creative applications of research data. Opposing viewpoints are tolerated and even nurtured in order to provide new solutions for old problems. Creative tension is part of the culture and is continuously encouraged in the belief that it leads to new lateral thinking within the organisation.

It is important to note that new generation organisations encourage the development of concurrent projects — often aimed at conflicting objectives, but based on the same research findings. These projects inevitably compete for the same limited development funds. The rationale is that the organisational learning which flows from this process will produce superior products at lower cost.

Globalisation

A significant number of the participants in the project indicated the urgency to address the challenges of globalisation and the *global mindset*, as they expected a massive increase in the number of multi-national firms entering local markets.

Without exception, the leading two or three organisations in each of their respective industries reflected high levels of interest in the opportunities and threats associated with the advent of globalisation. Organisations such as Murray & Roberts, JCI, Barlows, Langeberg and Malbak, have shown considerable foresight in recent years in developing off-shore interests, and examining the underlying issues related to business practices in foreign environments. In contrast, an alarmingly high number of traditional-trend organisations appear to have been caught flat-footed by the accelerating pace of South Africa's re-entry into the international markets. These organisations are faced with three primary challenges:

- The lack of internationally experienced managers — "think local but act global";
- The lack of a venturing approach, especially on foreign soil; and
- The lack of know-how on establishing sound international strategic alliances rather than *strategic flings*.

Recent trends indicate that today's multi-national firms will be superceded by the "relationship enterprise". This is a network of strategic alliances among big businesses, spanning different industries and countries, but held together by common priorities and goals which encourage them to act almost as a single business. Current examples are the extended alliances developing in airlines SAA/American Airlines, and BA/US Air; the automotive industry Honda/Mercedes Benz, Ford/Mazda, Toyota/GM; and the computer industry Microsoft/Compaq.

The rapid increase in cross-border alliances between firms in recent years has encouraged management scientists to develop the concept of the *virtual organisation* (discussed in the following section). Emerging trends suggest that future global organisations will form strategic alliances around specific market opportunities which lie beyond the technological, organisational, political or financial reach of any one of the alliance partners.

Among South African multi-nationals such as Anglo American Investment Corporation, Sasol, Engen, Liberty Life, RandCoal, SA Breweries, Dorbyl and others, there is an urgent need to develop a multi-functional and *multi-skilled* pool of true international managers. South African organisations, when extending their operations internationally, are faced by the challenge of operating a "capsule head office". This is a highly mobile, much reduced complement of internationally competent managers who are able to augment any particular aspect of the line operations at a moment's notice. The lack of a permanent home-base in exchange for a multiple set of home countries is known to cause substantial psychological imbalance for the unprepared executive. Therefore, as more and more organisations face the task of creating organisational synergy across cultural, national, and economic borders, managers have to be able to act locally but think internationally, grasp global issues and opportunities and cope with the resulting stress levels.

The virtual organisation

A virtual organisation is defined as a system which has the capability of perpetually adapting to the needs of the customer. Products which are developed by virtual organisations are characterised by the intense involvement of the customer in their original development. New generation organisations in South Africa, while still lagging behind major international counterparts, are now indicating an urgency in institutionalising the philosophy of virtuality. In this regard two aspects need to be considered.

First, there needs to be involvement by all employees in reading, interpreting and causing action on market signals. An exciting new trend is the extent to which organisations now involve employees in sampling customer opinions, setting up analysis teams to enhance product/service processes, and manage feedback to assess customer reaction.

Second, it is important to insist on making customer concerns transparent to all divisions of the organisation, regardless of their function in the business. New generation organisations flourish because they understand the customer and customer concerns and disseminate this information throughout the entire organisation — the notion of being customer obsessed. Employees are encouraged to delve for further information regarding customer problems and market opportunities. The use of cross-functional groups to examine customer concerns and market opportunities are part of the customer focus pattern in these organisations.

Drivers and sources of learning

An interesting phenomenon in recent years is that the drivers and sources of organisational learning are converging. Contemporary developments in competitiveness show that continuous benchmarking and emulation of the outstanding best practices of competitors, suppliers, distributors, customer organisations and other industry leaders have become the norm for organisational learning. These developments have prompted new generation organisations to recognise that organisational learning is facing a crucible — the rate of organisational learning must proceed at the same

Figure 2. Drivers and sources of learning

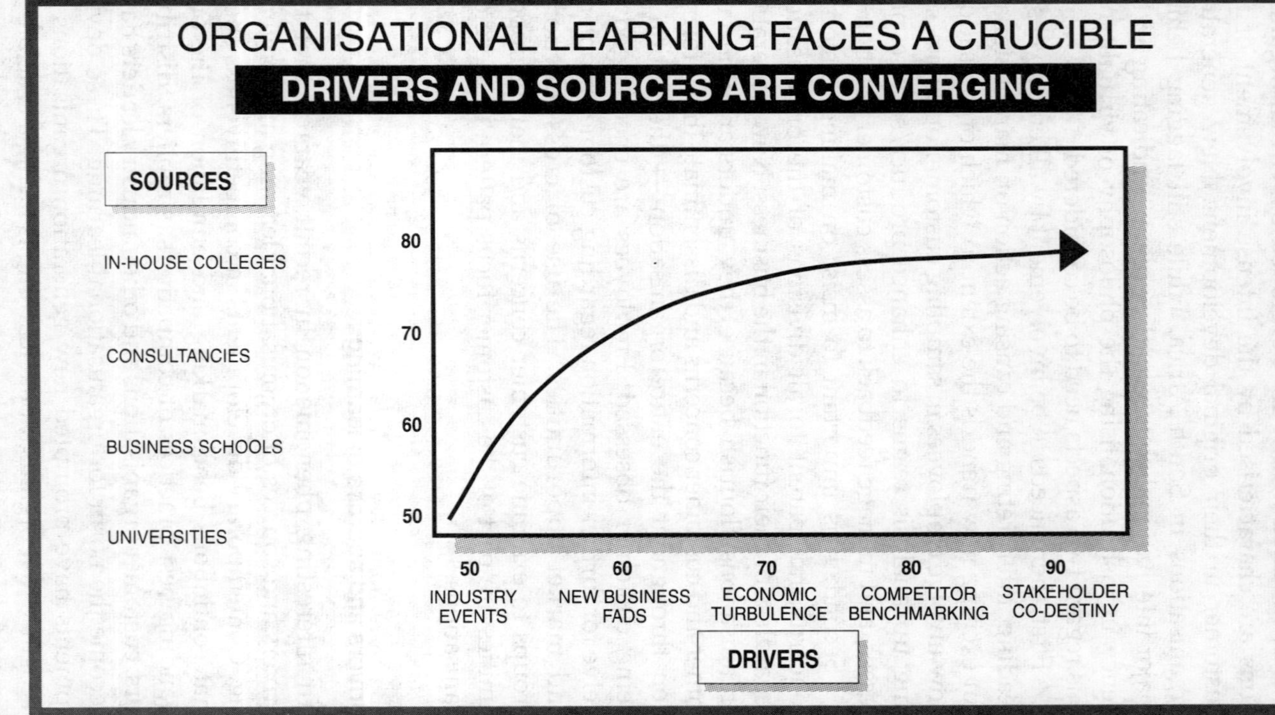

pace as environmental and competitive changes. In short, future organisational learning has little choice but to meet the demands of virtuality. This requires that new generation organisations ensure that their sources of learning are in tune with the drivers of organisational learning (see Figure 2).

Drivers

A major impediment has been the fact that many organisations have not distinguished between appropriate and inappropriate drivers of organisational learning. Organisational learning has been driven by the following forces:

Industry events

Many industry events have forced organisations to take notice, adapt or die. These include new technology breakthroughs such as interactive multi-media television through CD-ROM. Other significant events include the formation of mega-corporations through the forces of globalisation and the economies of scale achieved via global electronic highways. Sadly, few South African organisations truly understand the future impact of technological changes on their industries.

Organisational fads

A study by Pascale shows that a key driver in traditional-trend organisational learning has been the addiction to a continual cycle of new fads in attempting to achieve organisational optimisation. This includes such techniques as quality circles, the participative management philosophy and a host of others, to which South African organisations have unquestioningly committed millions of Rands. The short-term impact, but long-term negative consequences of slavishly following these fads has been more than apparent in recent years.

Economic turbulence

Economic turbulence has forced almost all organisations to re-examine themselves in terms of market related performance and comparative economic and competitive industry norms. The research indicates that a surprisingly high number of South African organisations are still "shooting in the dark". Many resist an in-depth self-examination against norms such as those developed for the benchmarking of performance.

Competitor benchmarking

In fast-moving industries such as health care, consumer electronics, travel and leisure, businesses are compelled to keep up with the emerging practices of industry leaders. Such leaders have developed a level of technological proficiency and customer orientation which enable them to change the competitive rules overnight. However, the research shows that many South African organisations are still lacking a grasp of the need to benchmark their competitors. The lack of in-depth competitive intelligence on the capability of competitors to revitalize themselves from the presently depressed levels, is alarming.

Stakeholder co-destiny

Co-destiny is a descriptive term currently popularised to describe the sense of interconnection of the various relationships between organisations, suppliers, distributors and end-users.

The virtual organisation is described as a meta-corporation where its sphere of influence extends upwards and downwards through all the components of the value-chain. It is suggested that all stakeholders have willingly entered a marriage of convenience, where a measure of mobility and freedom is exchanged for a measure of predictable survivability and shared benefits.

Too few South African organisations have fully grasped the benefits of *stakeholder co-destiny*. Co-destiny has implications for the nature of the learning relationship between stakeholders. The main characteristic in the new generation organisation is the extent to which it outsources non-core activities on the basis of mutual trust and reliability. Furthermore, all stakeholders realise that the network is no more than a constellation of psychological commitments, almost like a magnetic field. New generation organisations tend to go to extraordinary lengths to ensure a level playing field in the learning process for their stakeholders.

Sources of learning

In recent years the sources of organisational learning have faced a substantial paradigm shift about their competitive advantages and value-added abilities. In most case, the institutions that offer organisational learning services have lagged behind the impact of environmental and competitive changes. In recent years however, many have moved from a purely inward-looking approach, towards a position of inter-dependence with the drivers of learning — particularly with respect to developments on benchmarking, competitor best practices, technological trends, and organisational fads. The caveat for South African organisations is to be very selective about outsourcing organisational learning services.

Business schools

The advent of business schools in the 60s was a response by universities to focus more directly on the emerging need for business-specific knowledge. Pressures from the business community as well as the current international economic turbulence are forcing academic institutions to re-assess their roles as teachers, change agents and purveyors of ideas. A major dilemma for business schools is the realisation that newly emerging technologies such as inter-active multi-media electronic networks will largely erode the proprietary monopoly they have traditionally enjoyed. It is critical to realise that many of the traditional business school methods have become defunct and need radical refurbishing if they are to remain viable.

Corporate colleges

In response to the need for more customised learning, many South African corporations have established sophisticated in-house colleges. The results have been less spectacular than expected. Unless these institutions can adapt continuously to the ever-changing focus in the marketplace they will not be able to deliver the type of relevant education and skills which are necessary for causing quantum leaps within the organisation.

Consultant services

There is an increasingly critical examination of the cost-effectiveness and value-adding capabilities of consulting services in South Africa. The reasons are two-fold.

First, years of sanctions and isolation have excluded many local consulting firms from international exposure on organisational competitiveness.

Second, consultants are often victims of myopia, caused by their narrow functional disciplines. Many corporate solutions on the other hand require quantum leap thinking to ensure the maximum effect in the value-chain.

New generation organisations, for the reasons discussed above, have found alternative means of gaining insight into industry trends and resolving complex internal problems. A popular approach appears to be the formation of informal contact networks among industry peers in South Africa, where ideas and information about trends are exchanged. For example, Human Resources managers in organisations have been pressured by recent socio-political developments to examine affirmative action and equal opportunity programmes more carefully. Wary of repeating well-publicised past mistakes, HR managers are now liasing with industry-related associations and business and labour bodies to find common solutions. In addition, some are now gaining additional mileage from forming best practices forums with the aim of establishing informal briefings on key issues, such as affirmative action programmes. Significantly, many of these activities are proving a more viable alternative to the conventional and orthodox forums of the established business consulting services.

Finally, an interesting development is the advent of business professionals who become manager-consultants. Senior managers with substantial experience, are commissioned by organisations in other industries to perform part-time consulting services in their areas of speciality. It provides a valuable and far less costly alternative to many businesses whose limited financial resources prevent them from hiring external specialists. In addition, this provides a reciprocal benefit to the organisation whose specialist manager gains experience by being exposed to different industry settings and framebreaking solutions.

Focused growth from the core

One of the key issues which has been neglected with regard to focused growth is the *locus of control*. The question is whether the locus of control in counter-trend organisations is different from that in traditional-trend organisations. That is, do these organisations reflect an internal or external locus of control?

In new generation organisations the focus is on an internal locus of control, i.e. to be in charge of one's own destiny. This approach challenges several conventional assumptions about the elements which determine corporate missions. For instance, the business mission of new generation organisations is primarily governed by strategic intent, and is not compromised by a narrow focus on historical capital outlay decisions or irrational management aspirations.

Managers in traditional-trend organisations however, acknowledge that the source of strategic intent in their organisations is a combination of:

- Ensuring optimum returns from capital spent on existing infrastructures;
- Management aspirations; and
- Capitalising on market opportunities.

Organisations often find it difficult to cut their losses on capital projects that did not succeed due to poor historical decisions. Far too often there is a substantial emotional issue about parting with bad investments.

The aspirations of the founding members, shareholders, or core management group as a key determinant of business mission should not be underestimated. Many participating organisations indicated a propensity for perpetuating the historical aspirations of the previous leadership beyond the scope of competitive logic. For example, the research indicated that para-statal organisations, previously state-owned monopolies and long-time industry giants often struggled to relinquish the mindset which presumed invincibility given their enormous size.

Executives in large organisations such as Transnet, Eskom and Sasol acknowledged the negative conditioning resulting from managing large corporate assets over an extended period. Faced with outsourcing or downsizing decisions, many senior managers admitted a deep psychological attachment to traditional assets and the difficulty of changing the focus or their way of working. It is noteworthy that the primary revenue streams in businesses such as Sasol Waxes and Viamax now come from sources very different from those on which their parent organisations, respectively Sasol 1 and Transnet, were built. In the case of Viamax the management has transformed the traditional view of logistics into one of supply chain management, moving from a dependency on visible assets (trucks, sheds, warehouses) to the intangible assets of intellectual know-how (integrated systems application, leading industry thinking, process management).

An important factor is that in new generation organisations focused growth is governed by *just-in-time-focus* (JITF). The strategies of organisations such as ABI, McCarthy Retail, Afcol and others, have made them masters of focused growth. Their essential focus is one of market opportunism and using a JITF approach on a continuous basis. This JITF approach ensures their ability to expand their core business by identifying new opportunities and leapfroging the competition into new domains. While this approach is well recognised internationally, South African organisations have not shown the same degree of agility and opportunism exhibited by such global leaders as Honda, GE, Panasonic, SAS, Sony and Microsoft.

South African organisations are learning painful lessons about ill-conceived strategies and unfocused growth. Such eminent business leaders as Amic's Spencer Sterling and McCarthy Retail's Clive Weil — both formidable turn-around strategists — believe that managers often go on acquisition trails because they are bored with the success formula of the core business. The glamour of new horizons too often becomes a major temptation and dramatically affects the performance of the core business. Other organisations that have been successful at acquisition such as SAB, Burhose, McCarthy Retail, and Kohler support the view that managers tend to lose their focus on the inherent success factors of a core business, as a result of their involvement in take-over detail, or boredom with the original success formula of the core business.

New generation organisations ensure focused growth in a particular way. The concept of focus in the business is viewed on three levels.

- At the corporate level the issue is about achieving optimised returns from the existing capital investment while creating new future investment opportunities.
- At the business level the issue is to maintain an optimum focus on the important management variables that form

the backbone of the business. The key success factors at the business level comprise a specific set of measures to assess the performance of the management to create economic value.

- At the sub-unit or departmental level the issue is to optimise the core competencies on which the customer encounter depends. The focus at the departmental level is on speed and simplicity of the workflow methods, control systems and management processes in the value-chain, and on ensuring the self-confidence required of an enquiring mindset to continuously overhaul the *value-chain*.

New generation organisations are substantially more focused than their traditional-trend counterparts, especially at the corporate level. The key success factors at this level are a balanced focus between a value-added role for the head office and an intensive effort to develop new investment horizons against a fixed time-frame. This requires a very specific set of benchmarks against which the corporate head office departments are measured in order to ensure a balance between internal and external focus for creating value.

This mixed role demands that corporate executives have a keen ability to focus sequentially on their internal and external concerns. New generation organisation executives excel at constantly shifting their attention from a wide, macro-focus on external opportunities, to a narrow, micro-focus on a limited set of internal variables within the existing core business.

It is this need for a balance between a diverging and a converging focus that requires the corporate executive to extricate himself from the *clutter* of the business. This however, creates a dichotomy in the sense that the need for distance from operational clutter during sensitive stages of a new corporate venture, is in conflict with the need for hands-on leadership from the executive.

Competing on customer worth

In recent years there has been a subtle shift in the competitive posture of emerging industry leaders. Project research confirms that new generation organisations are starting to compete on *customer worth*, instead of competing on relative value-added. The definition of customer worth is the net difference between perceived benefits and perceived costs (negatives) of doing business with an organisation. (See Figures 3 and 4.) The perceived benefits of a customer encounter include many tangible and intangible factors, such as price, location, variety, service, reputation, goodwill and fit between customer needs and the purchased product. Similarly perceived costs (negatives) include both tangible and intangible factors such as poor quality, defects, low service levels, product complexity and unreliability. Comparative perceptions play a significant role in establishing customer worth.

First, one particular factor may be perceived as a benefit or a cost (negative). For example, a customer looking for a budget-price product may perceive the price of a product to be a benefit when doing business with organisation A, until the customer discovers organisation B is offering lower prices on the same range of products. Whether the price of product A is still a good budget price has lost its relevance to a large extent.

Second, perceptions of worth are the net result of a differential increase or decrease in either one or both of the two dimensions — perceived benefits or perceived costs. The net perceived worth of a product may not increase at all if the customer's perceptions of bad service increases — even although the organisation has spent substantial amounts to improve the product quality.

The key difference between the customer worth approach of new generation organisations and the value-added approach of traditional-trend organisations is that customer worth strategies allow all employees an opportunity to improve the competitive capabilities of the organi-

Figure 3.　Customer worth – small value

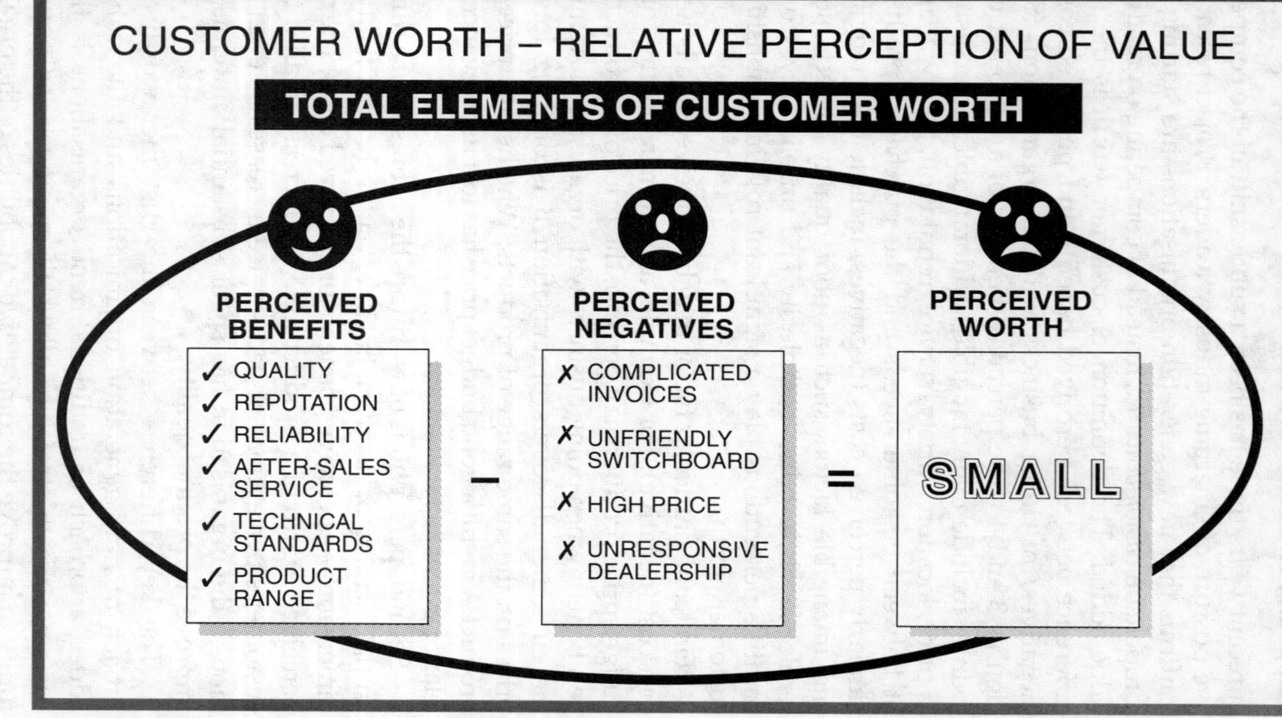

sation. Adding more perceived value to a range of products inevitably requires capital investment decisions which involve a substantial amount of management attention. The improvement of perceived worth means that the organisation has a choice. It can achieve its objective by focusing on either:

- The perceived benefits side of the equation (such as decreasing price, adding product functionality, or increasing the service network).
OR
- The perceived costs side (such as decreasing paperwork required of the new customer, eradicating non-value adding activities in the value-chain of workflow, decreasing non-mandatory expenses and eliminating poor interdepartmental communication to resolve customer queries).
OR
- The organisation can choose a combination of the two. The point is that the latter does not require significant capex decisions, but rather compels every employee to get involved.

It is therefore not suprising that organisations that respond to market share losses with purely benefit-adding strategies, often fail to achieve optimum employee involvement, since employees seldom see themselves as being involved to the extent of authorizing additional benefits.

The findings show that new generation organisations make the gap between present and desired levels of perceived customer worth transparent to all those involved in creating the value-chain. The focus is on forming inter-functional process teams for the specific purpose of concentrating on particular customer segments. The objective is to examine customer perceptions of worth, areas of opportunity, and concerns about present products and future requirements. These teams have the power to involve their counterparts from distributors, customers or supplier or-

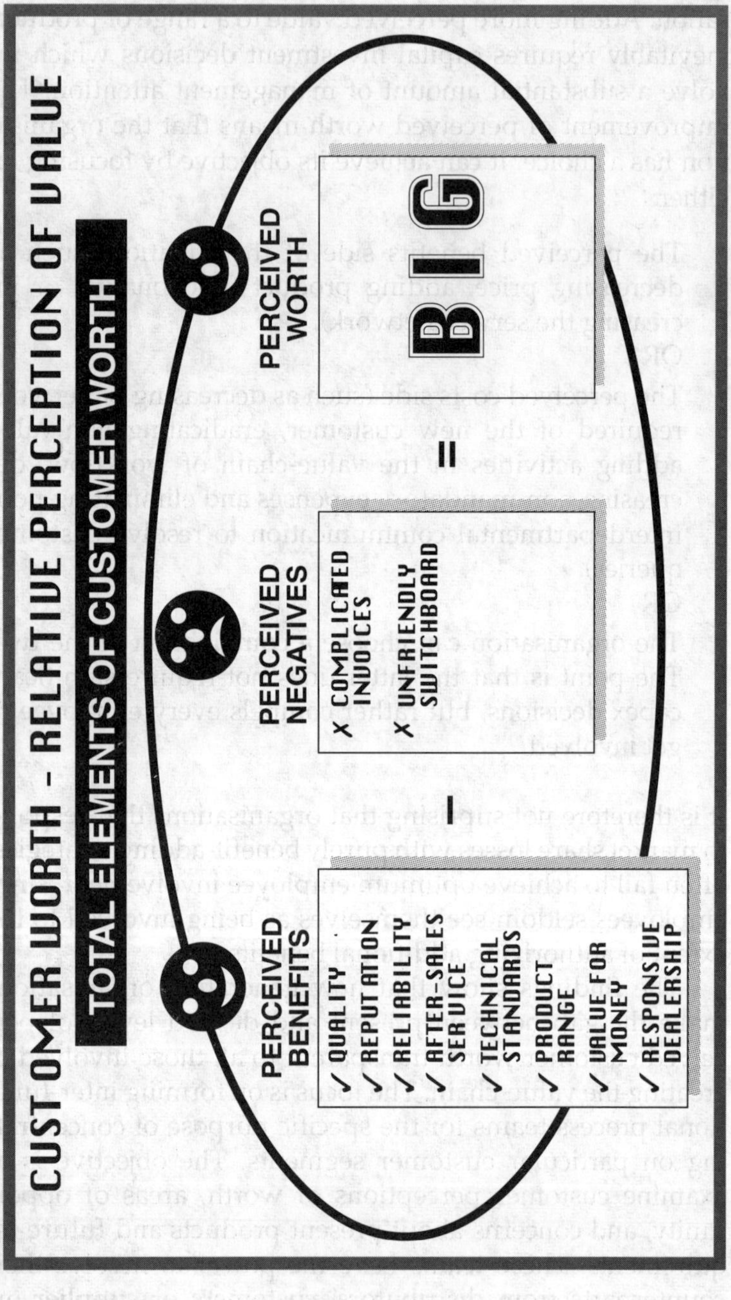

Figure 4. Customer worth – big value

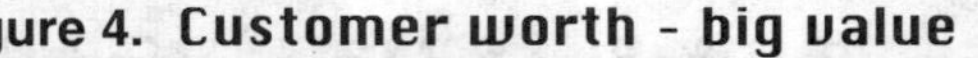

ganisations, draw up recommendations and implement corrective strategies. A characteristic of the customer process teams employed today in several organisations, is the extent to which management "gets out of the way" after communicating these customer concerns to their employees. The employees are formed into teams for the purpose of resolving these customer concerns, and more often than not, end up *rattling the cages* of many divisions within the organisation. These teams develop substantial skills in translating and transmitting customer concerns to the entire value-chain inside the organisation, and show considerable competence in improving the decision processes and job tasks that drive the workflow through the value-chain. This often leads to a re-engineering of the functioning of the organisation.

CHAPTER FIVE

Mobilising capability

The hallmark of the new generation organisation is the extent to which it purposefully mobilises its competitive capabilities to achieve aspirations beyond the conventional reach of its existing resources.

Whereas many organisations excelled at managing process in the 80s, the challenge of the 90s will be purposeful leadership across the entire organisation. The previous decade was noted for an over-application of process-related corrective strategies. Today it is recognised that work which is not meaningful for employees and which serves little purpose in creating customer value is often the cause of lack of competitiveness. It is, therefore, critical that particular attention is paid to deploying employee talent and energy in such a way that they become meaningful and constructive.

Harvard's Prof. Levitt summarises the challenge for counter-trend organisations in the following statement : "Organisations exist to enable ordinary people to do extraordinary things. Most of the world's work gets done, and with remarkable dependability, through organisations that routinise the process of doing their work. Precisely because of that, the purpose for which organisations exist cause organisations to decline in their ability to achieve their purpose. Routinisation of anything is self-effacing. It deadens alertness, attentiveness, imagination, energy and reaction time. Wherever routine reigns, special effort is needed to sustain attention and responsiveness, to energise the system and its functionaries, to freshen the mind, and get people moving.... The effectively functioning organisation makes change its open ally. It keeps the barriers low. Its leaders know that survival depends on the regular euthanasia of the organisation's regularities. Otherwise everybody and everything winds down. Entropy overtakes enterprise. Competitiveness diminishes and finally expires."

PRINCIPLES FOR MOBILISING CAPABILITY

Project research has identified three principles in mobilising capability:

- Defy the old paradigms;
- Focus on speed, simplicity and self-confidence; and
- Create an obsession with perpetual renewal.

Principle 5: Defy the old paradigms

New generation organisations are masters of discontinuous strategic thinking. The source of their competitiveness lies in their ability to defy the logic of conventional wisdom and leapfrog traditional culture in favour of brand new ways of doing things. Old paradigms have to be broken down before new perspectives can arise and flourish. It is almost a case of burying the old before creating the new.

In recent years there have been an increasing number of organisations caught flat-footed by the rapid political and commercial change in South Africa. They appear to have been incapable of rejecting their long-held assumptions about strategic direction and competitive advantage. They changed only incrementally and on an ad hoc basis, largely because past successes came about by doing more of the same. These organisations could be in jeopardy, since they continue to practise the approaches of the 60s and 70s. These approaches were relevant in their time, but as the pace of change accelerated, a complete re-think of the assumptions that have characterised South African organisations and their competitive success, has become necessary. Presently these organisations face major upheavals due to the introduction of last resort corrective strategies. Such strategies range from downsizing and rationalisation, to the more drastic merger and take-over activity that has become common in South Africa during the last five years. The argument in favour of discontinuous thinking is best illustrated by a number of examples.

A prime example of incisive, discontinuous yet holistic thinking about meeting market demands is found in the Afrox group. Its Chairman, Peter Joubert, has developed a reputation among business peers, analysts and subordinates for unconventional thinking. For many years the organisation has been hallmarked as a lateral-thinking business. Its expansion from the traditional gases and welding business into hospitals and health care, has been framebreaking to say the least. Critics of its shift in strategy have now become its most ardent supporters. With hindsight it has been a remarkable strategy, given the state of flux in its industries, and the opportunity for downstream integration. Significantly, the move was seen as both risky and unorthodox in the engineering sector.

Managers at Afrox are fond of relating how its Chairman not only challenged the traditional wisdom of his executives, but was also able to bring new insights to the way Afrox ran its business. All it needed, according to Peter Joubert, was the necessary will to win and the determination to go through a sharp learning curve in order to succeed. This gift for lateral and unconventional thinking has made Afrox a dominant performer on the JSE and certainly a leader in the engineering sector in South Africa. This discontinuous strategic thinking has highlighted the shortcomings of many old paradigms within Afrox.

Regarding the issue of corporate structure and job responsibilities, Afrox has achieved startling paradigm shifts. With its typically unorthodox approach to doing things Afrox introduced the so-called *amoeba structure*. This structure which has been utilised successfully over many years, defies the traditional practice of conventional job descriptions and accompanying job boxes which so many corporate executives find themselves in. Instead, Afrox is seen as essentially a *horizontal organisation* operating on the basis of value-chains.

The concept of the organisation as an *amoeba* — a living organism in which the component cells (tasks and jobs) grow, adapt or shrink, according to environmental conditions and situational demands — has become a major talking point in South African businesses. The idea was pioneered by Joubert, and has become a major point of focus among organisations searching for second generation solutions to solving the problems of specialisation and functional task entrenchment. This kind of entrenchment has resulted in the problem of creating corporate chimneys within vertical functional structures. The amoeba approach implies that there is a great deal of flexibility and horizontal focus in the business and that, through multi-skilling, no individual is left to stagnate in any one division or domain. Employees own their jobs, in as much as they are empowered to re-create their jobs as the situation demands, without rigid adherence to a set of job descriptions reminiscent of large bureaucracies. Horizontal adaptability is also an important key to the success of the amoeba approach. This means co-opting whatever help and advice is needed from other divisions within the organisation.

What is important about the amoeba structure in Afrox is its ability to change the traditional practices regarding the allocation of responsibility based on experience level, status and managerial expectation. The structure is focused on the notion of creating *knowledge champions* throughout the business. Although the format may be a little different, the approach followed by CMI Rustenburg, Toyota, Spescom, C.G. Smith Sugar, FreeGold, Randfontein Estates, the CSIR, ISG, and Rustenburg Plats, resembles the thinking of an amoeba structure. In all these organisations the traditional paradigms have been shifted dramatically. They continue to move people from one part of the organisation to another, from one level to another, and from one experience base to another. The traditional acceptance of corporate chimneys does not hold water for these organisations. It is interesting to find that multi-skilling within these organisations is an accepted norm. This creates a host of opportunities in terms of the type of career ladders than now become available to employees. For instance, the newly appointed Chief Operating Officer in the Engen Group is not a traditional petroleum executive, but comes from a mining background and has become multi-skilled over the years. This also applies to the new Chief Executive for the Afrox Group, who is not from an engineering, but an accounting background. Executive multi-skilling has enabled the new CEO to understand every aspect of the major engineering conglomerate he now heads.

There are many other examples of major paradigm shifts in South African organisations. ABI, the major softdrink producer in South Africa, was recently forced into a position in which its whole distribution network in the black townships was in jeopardy. By using a fairly unconventional approach of *hanna-hanna* with the local community and civics, it was able to create an *indigenous* solution which worked very well for the business. This solution dictated that ABI depart from the traditional practice of moving its products through the conventional distribution routes and instead use containers as depot points at the entrances to the townships. From there runners would be used to distribute the product into these territories. This obviated the need for ABI vehicles to travel into the townships. Another innovation from ABI has been the introduction of cooler trays supplied to vendors in order to move its product into territories where there has been strong competition from its opposition canners and bottlers of softdrinks.

Another example of the extent to which these organisations reject a rigid adherence to conventional paradigms, is the approach to the human resourcing structure of the business. Whereas the human resource division is traditionally located at the head office and is highly centralised, in these counter-trend organisations the centralised HR position is becoming obsolete. Line managers are being made responsible for being their own HR and IR practitioners, using head office support only on policy and critical matters.

The turnaround in the Southern Sun Group is an example of analytical thinking which has defied all the paradigms related to running a hotel chain. Faced with the worst possible trading conditions in many years, the group has embarked upon a highly innovative approach for regaining strategic initiative in the marketplace. When the Group Managing Director, Ron Stringfellow, launched a process of restructuring the Southern Sun Group, he recognised that a resurrection of this group was dependent on a bold, creative and yet simple strategy. This is almost identical to the thinking applied by Mike Sander of AECI. It involved restructuring the Group into independent business units and offloading those units that were no longer seen as being part of the core business. In both these organisations the *big divide* which existed between head office and the operations was eliminated in favour of a highly co-operative style between these two elements in the corporate structure.

Foodcorp is yet another example of a major restructuring and resurrection. Dirk Jacobs in his bid to make Foodcorp a viable business used all the formulas of decentralisation, autonomy, independent business responsibilities and an understanding of future markets. Lion Match in its approach to its problematic business used much the same kind of approach. CEO Ted Turner used a combination of exhaustive analysis combined with strategic insight and opportunism to refocus the match, white appliances, cutlery and a number of other diverse businesses in the Group. All have been restructured on decentralised lines according to specific market niches.

Stringfellow recognised the divisive power of introducing radically new ideas into an industry which, although it appears very colourful and entrepreneurial, is essentially traditionalist. An example is the ingenious way in which facts, assumptions and projections were unemotionally scrutinised to develop the now famous concept of the hotel brands. The hallmark of the new Southern Sun Group strategy is its simplicity and conceptual appeal. The branding approach was used to segment the hotels according to customer requirements.

Prospects for future survival begged a radical overhaul of the Southern Sun Group's strategy in order to "stay alive till 1995", the projected beginning of the next major upswing of tourism for South Africa. The key challenge was to improve profitability by significantly improving the total room-yield of the Group's entire range of hotels. Two factors proved to be key constraints:

- The escalation of the fixed cost structure had to be rapidly broken down into managable, bearable cost chunks; and

- The ability to deliver value at reasonable prices for the wide range of domestic and international market segments had to be improved dramatically.

Not suprisingly, Stringfellow concluded that management's assumptions regarding their understanding of customer requirements needed a *zero-based* review. Management could not afford to hold onto the outdated philosophies of its predecessors, who had been operating in a time of good trading conditions, easy shareholder pockets and less demanding customers. Southern Sun was faced with a basic choice:

- Rationalise, squeeze remaining assets, tighten control, square up to the unions to lessen their grip on margins, and keep one's head down until things improve, because that's the way it's been done in the past.

  OR

- Boldly adjust one's view of how a future hotel group should function, radically alter the composition of customer offerings, drive down controllable costs, drive up quality and value for money, and view labour, suppliers and customers as stakeholders.

Probably the most complex part of the solution for Southern Sun, Foodcorp, AECI and Lion Match was to find a formula that would offer improved quality, provide more value for money and gear the range of customer offerings to the various market segments.

The conclusions drawn from the analyses conducted by these organisations was that the concept of the value-chain had to become the standard philosophy. The focus of each business and its various departments was to become more customer-orientated and concentrate on creating value for every customer segment. This required a shift from the traditional focus on functional specialisation towards a more integrated process-flow of services across functional departments. The challenge for a typical management team was to overcome the traditional departmental differences in culture, work ethic, workflow procedures and differential approaches to measuring and rewarding performance.

In the case of Southern Sun, management realised that this required a change in the portfolio of the hotels. In addition, the operating structure had to accommodate a more businesslike approach. The new branding strategy was developed to cater for all sectors of the hotel industry providing clear brand offerings for different customer segments. Once the underlying logic had been accepted, Stringfellow used this to overhaul many of the remaining inconsistent paradigms in the Southern Sun philosophy.

Two outstanding examples of paradigm shifts in the thinking of the abovementioned organisations are outlined below. In both cases innovative, bold thinking provided the framework for creative solutions, the kind of discontinuous strategic thinking referred to earlier.

- It was generally accepted that the business had to shift from a primarily fixed-cost structure towards one that favoured variable costs. This is the old dilemma of traditionally labour-intensive organisations. The problem was resolved by a two-pronged approach in which the groups shifted their employment policy from one of specialisation towards multi-skilling. Employees were retrained to cope with several task outputs required during a convential shift of work. The focus was on enlarging job ownership. This led to a more constructive relationship between management and the workforce and produced a substantial value-added contribution to the bottom-line. At no time did management compromise its position in this regard. It was a case of *FIFO* — fit in or fly off.

- The next major innovation was to resolve the predicament of providing a level of quality service at a price the customer could afford. In the case of Southern Sun the quality of the bedroom is a critical factor in the customer's mind. Management approached the issue of the bedroom in a very different way. Employing discontinuous strategic thinking, they invited customers to an exhibition of mock-up bedrooms to provide their views on the suitability of the design, construction and furnishings for new and existing hotels. Foodcorp used a similar approach in a direct interface with the customer at the supermarket level, with the focus on creating affordable food products.

In all these Groups a brand new corporate culture was needed. Head offices were reduced in size and political status. The focus was moved from the vertical to the horizontal, both in terms of power and decision-making processes, through a devolution of power. A key shift in the culture was the development of a collaborative approach with all stakeholders. For example, the chief executives in all these organisations were on record as seeing labour unions as part of the solution, rather than adversaries. They were nevertheless tough in demanding from unions a shift towards a collaborative approach to ensure a joint future.

Principle 6: Focus on speed, simplicity and self-confidence

General Electric (GE) has, since the middle 80s provided an international example of successful, large-scale organisational renewal. Relentlessly driven by the visionary Jack Welch, GE has been able to transcend limitations of size, product diversity and sophisticated management processes in its quest for re-emerging as the dominant international player in its particular market sector. It has, in fact, emerged as an organisation which has the characteristics of being small, maneouverable and responsive, while harnessing the benefits of large scale financial and political clout. Underlying the renewal of GE, Welch used his famous war cry of "speed, simplicity and self-confidence" to rally the organisation around the challenges required of a dominant player. He removed the entrenched *mumbo jumbo* which caused retarded responses to many decision processes within GE.

The essence of speed is in the response to market situations, provision of correct information where it is required, making decisions, and eliminating obsolete practices and policies. Simplicity is reflected in clarity of strategic intent, formal and informal communication, and in the organisational structure and management process, products and services. Self-confidence is reflected in the willingness to challenge traditional conventions; to move away from the internal inward-looking focus towards a more externally oriented approach, to develop an enquiring culture and create a level of openness towards all stakeholders.

An important indicator of the lack of competitiveness in South African organisations is typified by the cumbersome, inflexible manner in which they conduct their strategy-formulating processes. These processes often appear to be sophisticated and practical. However, closer examination reveals that they have become paperchase exercises — entwined with formality, clutter and routine documentation that is not pertinent to strategy. Project research found that the majority of managers in a random survey of five large South African organisations rated between 35% and 45% of the routine activities in their strategy planning and review cycles as being unproductive. Aspects such as meetings, reviews and documentation were regarded as being wasteful and failing to create any significant value for the customer base. Interestingly, each of these organisations had recently completed, or was engaged in, a major rationalisation drive. The underlying problem appeared to be that these organisations had removed people and jobs, without changing the historical routine prescribed by the job — the *corporate boxes* remained intact.

An important example of an organisation that searches for speed, simplicity and self-confidence is observed in SA Breweries. Key to the SA Breweries management philosophy is the cultivation of an on-going, dynamic review of their business direction and market actions. The Chairman and his executive view SAB as a simple business — one that should not be cluttered by bureaucratic controls and excesses. A good example of the low level of clutter relates to meetings and reports. The group has only four formal meetings scheduled per year and refuses to accept reports that are longer than two pages. The whole focus is on getting to the core of what the real strategic issues are all about. A strong reflection of this is the way in which SAB has excelled in "doing the right things, rather than doing things right". Whereas most organisations ignore this caveat for fear of appearing to be simple-minded, SAB's Chairman has a refreshingly simple approach to things which are complicated. He believes that while the SAB approach is less than perfect — and sometimes less rigorous than that which typical bureaucrats might strive for — what it loses in predictability and rigorousness, it gains in intellectual leadership, innovation, flexibility and response to the marketplace.

Similarly, groups such as American Swiss, Blue Circle, Portnet, and SA Nylon Spinners have all emphasised simplicity as being a key factor in ensuring a high degree of innovation and market responsiveness.

Self-confidence has always been a hallmark of the SAB group. It has been enormously successful over many years and has built a reputation for being a formidable competitor in those markets it chooses to dominate. The Beer Division, for instance, has a reputation for very rapid and flexible action in changing the rules in the marketplace within which it operates. It is a lot quicker off the starting blocks than most other large organisations. There is, according to its executives, a strong belief in the organisation's ability to create the future. In taking business risks, the Beer Division is able to distinguish between business decisions which are due to bad luck, and those that are due to bad judgement. It is well recognised inside the group that the marketplace is a risky one and that a propensity for calculated risk is imperative as part of the mainstream thinking. Therefore, SAB is optimistic about its ability to continue to dominate its marketplace, providing it can deliver what the customer wants at the right quality, at the right price and at the right time. Furthermore, SAB recognised many years ago the potential problem of corporate malaise and its accompanying corporate obesity and has done a great deal to control these diseases.

Steven Mulholland encountered a similar problem in taking over the Times Media Group in 1986, as did Dr John Job in taking over Sentrachem in 1991, and Barry Swart in taking over First National Bank in 1988. In all of these organisations the solution has been to introduce the notion of creative tension within the business. Such creative tension reduces complacency, introduces *corporate thunderstorms*, and ensures higher levels of candour. If, for instance, a bad *strategic call* is identified, these organisations' approach to formulating strategic action urges prompt corrective measures. They show no embarrassment about recognising shortcomings and dissecting the problem in order to prevent similar, negative occurrences in the future. The self-confidence inherent in their ability to dissect the problem and be self-critical is a hallmark of all these organisations. Says the Chairman of SAB: "We are actually arrogant enough to have confidence in what we do. We believe we are leaders, but we are also humble enough to know that we make mistakes. We can laugh at ourselves and our mistakes. If you are prepared to accept that, then you can do something about your mistakes".

Much has been achieved in eliminating *analysis-paralysis* or inflexible strategy-making from the fabric of SA Breweries, Times Media Limited, Sentrachem and First National

Bank. The following sentiment is reflected in one way or another by all the CEO's of these organisations: "Of course we make a lot of mistakes. But one of the hallmarks of our people is to recognise these and correct them as rapidly as possible. We try not to make the same mistakes again. This often means having to alter our strategy".

Principle 7: Create an obsession for perpetual renewal

New generation organisations recognise that organisational renewal is a journey and not a destination. They feel compelled to continuously search for improvements and frame-breaking ideas. An important finding of the research among new generation organisations is the view that the engine of renewal is driven by making customer concerns transparent to all areas of the organisation, while ensuring that corrective actions are governed by strong organisational values. They have discovered that the shortest route to renewing the way the organisation functions is through the combined chemistry of energising employees through a powerful set of corporate game rules or beliefs, while simultaneously making customer concerns the goal of the entire employee corps. While appearing to be deceptively simple, this discovery should not lull large organisations into underestimating the difficulty of continuously sustaining large-scale renewal.

A prime example is that of First National Bank. In its quest for re-emerging as the dominant force in the banking sector, First National Bank has focused its energy on getting back to customer basics. Led by Barry Swart, First National Bank has since 1989 relentlessly pursued the objective of achieving a quantum leap in creating customer value. Swart's vision is one of capturing the imagination of a selected client base. His point of departure has been to decrease the *organisational drag* associated with being a large technology-driven organisation, conditioned by risk-averseness and a predisposition for time-consuming routine and complicated procedures — typical of the traditional banking sector.

This prompted the top executives to make a conscious decision to rid the organisation of cumbersome organisational processes that did not create customer value. To achieve this it was important for the organisation to focus on a common set of values for all its employees (known as shared values). This strategy was also applied by Glynn Taylor of C.G. Smith Sugar, Errol Rutherford of Corobrik, Ken Dicks of Freegold, Ken Maxwell of Randfontein Estates, Duke Davidson of Portnet, Barry Davidson of Rustenburg Plats, Spencer Stirling of Samcor and Dr Anton Moolman of Transnet. This approach is intended to provide the framework which allows these organisations to ensure perpetual renewal within their various businesses, because it lies at the root of creating self-managing organisations.

A prime example of this obsession with perpetual renewal is the work that is currently being done to eliminate activities, procedures, policies and processes that create little or no customer value. Using a very focused renewal process, the aim is to get each of the organisations' employees to eliminate unnecessary bureaucracy in these large command-and-control type businesses. This is achieved by getting employees to take charge of their own jobs and use their creative initiatives in a way never previously condoned. In the case of First National Bank the ten-year vision is for each employee to have both the confidence and willpower to identify and remove anything that inhibits framebreaking attitudes, ideas and behaviour, for the benefit of customers. It is interesting to note that the chief executive has chosen two aspects to act as counter-balancing forces in liberating the organisation:

- Ensuring that the priorities of both the corporate and the operational levels are directed at customer concerns, everything else being peripheral; and
- Institutionalising a set of practical corporate beliefs or game rules (known as critical management factors) as substitutes for the traditional role of the manager as final arbiter, controller and disciplinarian.

Highlighting customer concern areas is a key priority for all the organisations discussed above. This has ensured that customer issues have been moved to the top of the management agenda. It is important to note that once the customers' concerns became highlighted, there was a substantial decrease in the emphasis on formal routine, in favour of attending to a limited set of core customer concerns.

The significant challenge to the chief executives in the organisations discussed above, is to prepare the way for an enquiring culture among their managers. In the case of the mining organisations, Freegold, Rustenburg CMI, Randfontein Estates and Rustenburg Plats, the quest for perpetual renewal and creating an enquiring culture flies in the face of the traditional way of doing things. The ability of these executives to introduce this change means that they concentrate on issues with a high degree of determination and energy input. Long-standing conventions are overriden in favour of a new generation way of thinking. With C.G. Smith, Corobrik, First National Bank and Samcor shifting the paradigms from a conformist culture to continuously questioning the status quo was not an easy matter. Holy cows had to be overturned, fear of failure removed, and *off-the-wall* approaches used in putting in place the substantial paradigm shifts that were required. The same applies to Portnet which manages South Africa's harbours, and Transnet which is the biggest single provider of transportation in South Africa. Both of these have moved away from being purely state-owned, input-driven organisations, towards commercialised, output focused businesses. They had to apply a *head-above-the-parapet* approach to taking the kind of risks that were required to cause this dramatic transition. The successes achieved in all these businesses to date, indicates a substantial return-on-investment for the risks taken, energy exerted, and pain endured.

KEY CONSIDERATIONS IN MOBILISING CAPABILITY

New generation organisations have identified several key considerations in their quest for optimum utilisation of resources, assets and know-how.

These issues address factors of capability such as organisational structure, the value-chain, the role of the head office, *decision ownership*, and *succession planning*.

Structuring to create value

The advent of the concept of the horizontal organisation (developed by McKinsey), has introduced a new paradigm in the configuration of organisations. This concept reflects a dramatic departure from the conventional structure with its emphasis on steep hierarchies and vertical differentiation. The movement has been towards creating a horizontally integrated organisational structure. The main focus of the horizontal structure is to emphasise the primary work output requirements as determined by the customers' perception of worth.

The implication is that work should be driven by the expectations of the downstream business areas and not by the perceived expectations of the department manager. The horizontal organisation and value-chain concepts still have very limited application in South African organisations. This is clearly an area for concern and rapid action.

A major inhibitor of the competitive capability of South African organisations is the phenomenon of *functional myopia*. The impact caused by a limited horizontal focus in large vertically-structured businesses is often underestimated. This is particularly the case with the large, established, diversified organisations in manufacturing, chemicals, utilities and services.

Project research found that many of these organisations are presently intensifying the search for a new organisational configuration. The new architecture is intended to deal with such issues as pups with fleas, management complacency, a lack of competitive stamina, bureaucratic obesity, the *switch-board syndrome*, a divergence between the objectives of different vertically structured functions and the removal of work that does not create customer value but is driven by functional self-interest.

To illustrate the extent of this myopia the research identified several major traditional-trend South African organisations, for instance, retailing, financial services and chemical businesses, which suffer from the classical problems of out-dated corporate structures, and the use of traditional matrix designs in managing the key customer value output streams. In the case of one such organisation a destructive level of friction clearly existed between production, distribution and marketing — this notwithstanding several efforts in recent years to adopt a more functional design. The major line divisions are all characterised by burgeoning head office structures and a large *cone of uncertainty* relating to decisions within the organisation (see Figure 5). They all suffer from what Prof Martin Nasser calls *wind-tunnel alienation* due to the substantial geographic distances between the production plant, situated in South Africa, and its marketing departments in Europe and the Far East.

Furthermore, the introduction of sophisticated matrix designs to manage the multiple variables along the value-chain has compounded the original problem: managerial time is usurped by a paperchase and endless meetings. Few of the techniques introduced to streamline the interdependency between the core functions in the strategic value-chain have met with any success. The lack of commonly shared interests, continuity between policy-making and execution, and the inability to maintain business focus among the various functions, reflects the dilemma this organisation has in changing to a horizontal configuration.

In the case of a large traditional-trend financial services organisation, the perennial conflict of interest between the lending line and the sales divisions of the organisation is viewed as a fact of life, with no solution in sight. Efforts at

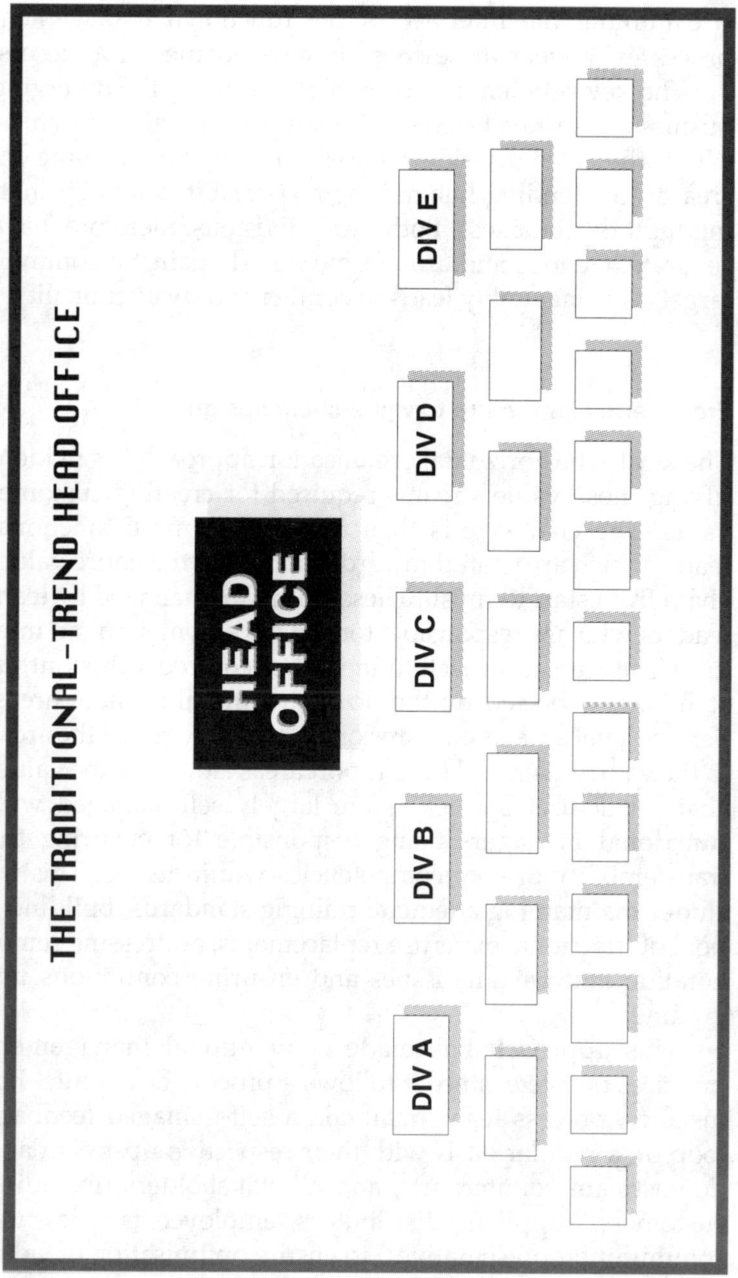

Figure 5. The traditional-trend organisation head office

streamlining the interface of the functional management processes between these divisions have not met with success.

The key problem has been highlighted as the diverging business priorities between the key functional hierarchies. While the sales division focuses on achieving volume increases, the lending line has the responsibility for eliminating high risk business. Both these divisions, therefore, have separate agendas and are not measured against a common target. This inevitably leads to conflict and dysfuctionality.

From vertical structure to value-chain design

The key to the horizontal organisation approach lies in identifying those value streams required for creating customer value. The challenge is then to establish multi-functional teams which are geared towards managing the entire value-chain from start to finish. These teams are managed by team leaders who are responsible for the development of an integrated process approach to meet the required value output standards expected by the downstream value-chain areas. Service level agreements are concluded between all the areas in the value-chain and the support areas alongside the value-chain structure. The teams are largely self-managed with functional managers being responsible for ensuring the transferability of core competencies within teams. This includes maintaining adequate training standards, building a pool of functional expertise replacements, addressing remuneration and benefits issues and ensuring continuous upgrading.

This approach has made conventional management practices obsolete, since it follows a process flow route. For instance, process teams maintain a self-managed feedback loop on a regular basis with their respective upstream and downstream counterparts, and all stakeholders (including customers, suppliers, distributors, employee families and community representatives) to ensure optimisation of value outputs and the upholding of stakeholder responsibilities.

Core competency training involves the entire base of the cross-functional team. In such organisations multi-skilling is aimed at deepening the core competency. This is in contrast to traditional-trend organisations where the aim in multi-skilling strategies is primarily to reduce the number of employees. In addition, annual upgrading training has been replaced with the concept of *just-in-time training*. The central focus is to train members of process teams as and when the skill is required. The *modus operandi* involves a number of factors:

- Team members are expected to maintain an increasing level of multi-skilling across functional disciplines;
- The value output teams are skilled at immediate and on-going transfer of best practices between all stakeholders and industry leaders; and
- Each team member is exposed to a regular in-depth core competency audit to determine strengths and weaknesses.

This ensures that the process team leader strikes a healthy balance between regular skill transfer and JIT training as and when the need arises.

Good examples of the kind of shifts that occur when an organisation moves from a vertical, functionally dominated structure towards a value-chain design, are the developments which have occured in Afrox, Shoprite-Checkers, Boart International, Eskom, Murray & Roberts, Edgars, AECI, Blue Circle, Times Media Ltd., Avis, Metropolitan Life, Santam and Sasol Waxes — all *profile players* within their respective sectors.

In these organisations it was determined that the best solution to improving the value-chain lay in overhauling the vertical functional structures in critical areas of the value-chain. This often involved restructuring traditionally separated functions such as customer services, accounts receivable, and technical support into an enlarged process team aimed at a distinctive market segment and delivering specific customer value outputs.

The boundaries between these functions are removed by establishing common value output areas, linked to specific performance standards, which are negotiated among team members and value-chain co-members, and checked with customers. Significantly, these changes are mostly identified, introduced and implemented by the employees, with managers often merely acting as facilitators.

An important development of the value-chain concept is the extent to which job ownership at the employee level has been resuscitated. Middle management has been deprived of real responsibility in recent years, hence the unfortunate shift towards greater task-focus and activity-centredness at the expense of customer value output improvements.

In organisations which adopt the horizontal approach, the shift from a task culture towards a value driven culture has been more than apparent. Conformance to job activity boundaries has been replaced by inquiry into the value creating capacity of day-to-day activities and procedures. This has meant the removal of the typical corporate boxes and the movement towards *bossless teams*. An important development is the rejection of the popular functional productivity and management by objective techniques of the 80s such as the establishment of task performance hierarchies established around functional key performance areas.

Probably one of the most significant changes in the approach of the value-chain design is the challenge of completely altering the way management disciplines the organisation. Many South African organisations have become disillusioned by well-intended employee liberalisation and democratisation processes. These processes, part of organisational renewal initiatives, have failed to noticeably increase the levels of accountability among employees.

In retrospect, by failing to go the whole way in restructuring the organisation into value-chains, these processes have not been effective in removing the invisible costs of conventional disciplinary techniques such as historical performance reviews. Most managers in most organisations spend the bulk of their time in meetings, producing reports checking systems, controls, procedures and regulations based on historical data, instead of on new issues, opportunities and priorities.

These processes have therefore not capitalised on the principles of value-chain design which enable management to concentrate on resolving emerging issues. In contrast the value-chain process and culture ensure that teams apply self-discipline in day-to-day decision activities. Traditional-trend processes have heightened employee expectations of increased decision-making discretion, without establishing the core competencies required for the efficient functioning of a value-chain structure.

In new generation organisations disciplining of employee performance and behaviour through traditional controls and procedures has been replaced by self-managed performance review sessions held regularly among peer teams in the value stream. During these sessions the respective process teams in the value-chain discuss and provide feedback to one another on the expected outputs and service standards (as agreed in the service level agreements). (See Figure 6.)

The most significant characteristic of jobs in the value-chain approach to organisational structure is that job design is the responsibility of the process team. In fact, some organisations have gone to extraordinary lengths to shift responsibility for job descriptions towards a combination of the individual employee, the process team and functional management.

The outcome of introducing the value-chain approach to organisational structure in South Africa has delivered promising results. Although the idea of the horizontal organisation is new to South African organisations, the project research found that substantial benefits could be gained from this approach.

Figure 6. New generation architecture – creating the value–chain

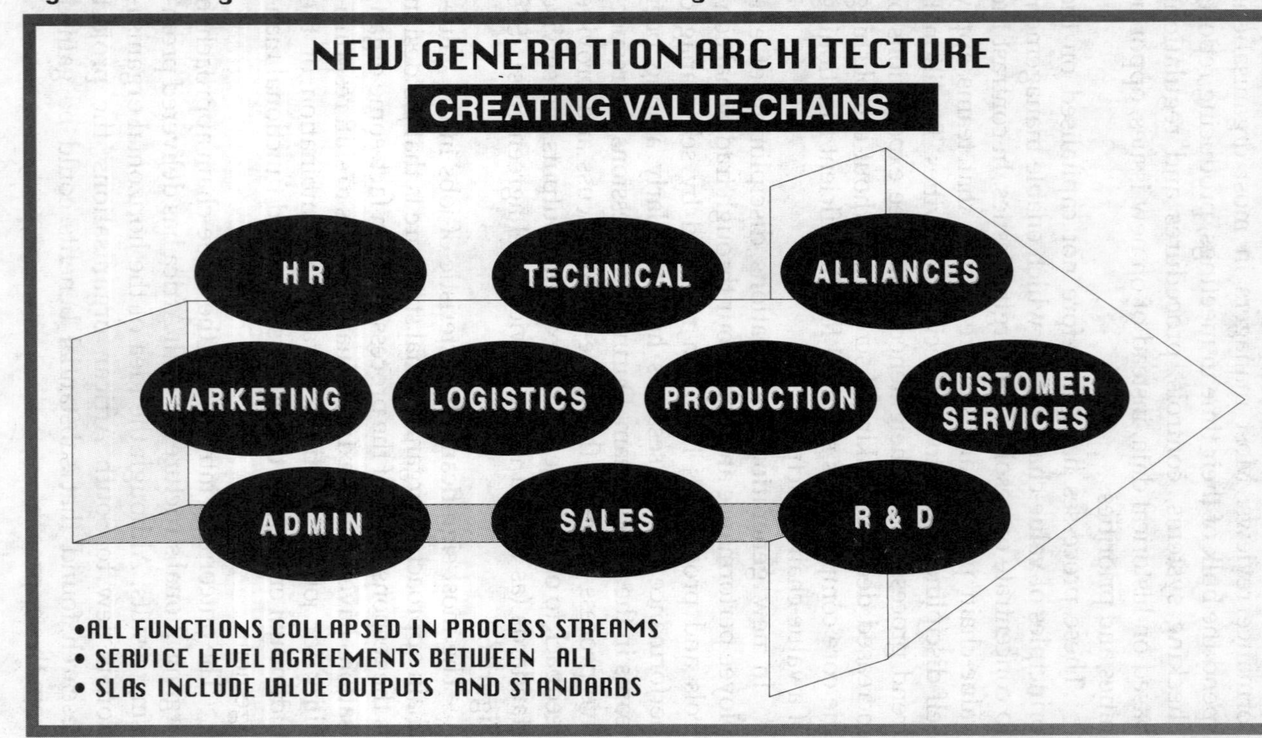

For instance, a new phenomenon of *edgelessness* or *seamlessness* has been identified as describing the close integration between the organisation, its suppliers, customers and distributors. The approach of Kohler Packaging illustrates this phenomenon of edgelessness. Their philosophy of co-destiny with all the stakeholders in optimising systems and integrating processes between Kohler and each supplier/customer has been a key factor in bonding suppliers and customers to the organisation. It has been achieved by:

- Re-engineering the supply chain;
- Creating opportunities for joint organisational learning through such initiatives as electronic data interchange (EDI); and
- Emphasising joint responsibility in striving for responsiveness and speed in the development of new products.

Rent-a-head office

The head offices of new generation organisations have been revolutionised. In terms of corporate stature, strategic planning, executive gamesmanship and office politics, a host of new rules and processes have emerged. These head offices have refocused their positions to ensure continuous corporate renewal, creating a level playing field, and providing the nerve centre of intellectual leadership in the organisation. The responsibility for budget achievement has been placed squarely on the shoulders of the various business units.

Project research indicates that there are a number of phases through which organisations have to pass in order to ensure a new style of head office.

- **Phase one:**
  The typical departure point is a corporate bureaucracy, highly dependent on its hierarchical and positional power for its functioning.
- **Phase two:**
  There is a move towards a streamlined, down-sized and trim head office — from corporate obesity to corporate

anorexia. In such a head office the corporate executives move away from their desks to interact with the operations in ensuring that the business is able to achieve optimised results and capitalise on new market opportunities.

- **Phase three:**
This is a phase in which the formation of a typical new generation organisation head office actually emerges. This is known as the *rent-a-head-office* (see Figure 7). It is characterised by lean, tight staffing — often no more than fifteen people for a large, diversified group — in which its central role is that of ensuring strategic focus, eliminating the politics and providing the necessary support to ensure that the business can function optimally. It encourages a type of federalism within the organisation with the head office being the co-ordinator of the various sovereign business areas. The move is towards a more *bossless organisation* in which the head office provides a concentration of *cerebral skills*, while the line is vested with the necessary operational skills. A significant feature of the new generation head office is that its *raison d'etre* is contained in a formal set of service agreements and standards, negotiated between the line operations and the head office support departments.

An important characteristic of this new style head office is that it is essentially self-funding. This approach is being used by Engen, Barlows Equipment Company, Foodcorp, Liberty Life, Edgars, Times Media, Randcoal, Southern Sun and Toyota.

Furthermore, instead of the traditional approach in which the head office is viewed as the political apex of the decision-making hierarchy, it becomes an integral part of the support system underlying the value streams in the strategic value-chain. It's focus is essentially that of orchestrating the various functions and divisions in such a way that it ensures optimised performance from the resources available. This is well illustrated by Pick 'n Pay, Southern Sun, Liberty Life and Engen.

Figure 7. The new generation "rent-a-head" office

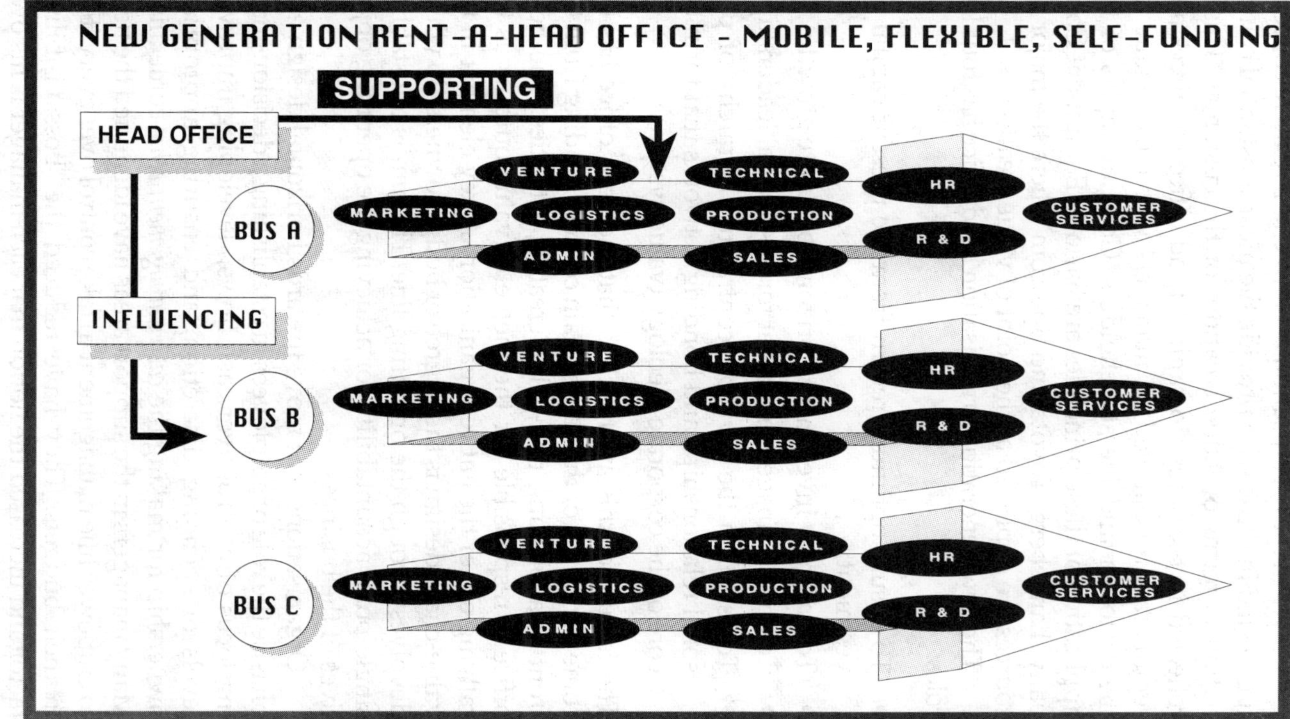

Power in the organisation is viewed as a relative concept. It is vested in those who provide the most substantial contribution in terms of value creation for the customer. This is reflected in the access to capital, head office resources and remuneration bestowed on managers who create value for the customer and the stakeholders. Good examples of the application of these principles are Barlows Equipment Company, Langeberg, Toyota and Spescom where the major resources are deployed at the point of value creation.

The new generation organisation head office has four key roles:

- To ensure optimum return from the present capital investment;
- To find new investment horizons for future growth;
- To build management talent for intellectual leadership;
- To establish the invisible contractual hierarchy of personal relationships and bonding networks that form the core of the corporate ideology (value system).

The feature of this approach is that the head office has become the driver of the value-chain concept, leading from the front in abolishing non-value creating activities. The head office is responsible for the theme of value outputs as the rallying cry of the entire organisation. A key element in the value-chain design is the degree of budget ownership which devolves through the operating line. The aim is to establish single-point acountability for achieving the operating objectives of the business.

Organisations that move towards horizontal design emphasise the role of employees in establishing a decision-making locus of control over cash flows, developing improved levels of spending discretion, and ensuring appropriate ownership for making the *cash management ethic* come alive. Many managers in the support areas have identified the need to empower line management to take control over every item in their budgets. They have reduced the "boss visibility" factor and increased the notion that each manager is his own man regarding budgets. Managers also identified the need to allow managerial involvement in the determination of corporate policies regarding the allocation of overheads which affect their operations. This simply means that instead of head office having the sole mandate for policy formulation the approach is now one of joint deliberation and ownership.

Three important ideas have emerged regarding the institutionalisation of budget ownership to the line:

- Managers within the head office and operational structure are assessed and remunerated on the achievement of a combination of individual and joint output objectives and service level performances. A type of *gain sharing* system based on the wealth creating capacity generated by these managers has been established.

- Line managers negotiate levels of required budgetary support in specific output terms with their support counterparts. The support manager retains only those budget items required for achieving the agreed value outputs. This is in contrast to the traditional practice where line managers do not have sufficient control over their own budgets. In addition, line operations in the new generation organisations use financial penalty mechanisms to address non-performance by support areas.

- The focus on profitability for business performance is now being replaced by cash flow measurement as the major indicator of business health. Project research has discovered that the historical focus has been on sales and bottom-line at the expense of sound cash flow measurement — being cash-smart. The revolt against the fixation on a narrow bottom-line focus has been led by Selwyn MacFarlane of SAB, Terry Rosenberg of McCarthy Retail, Dr John Job of Sentrachem, Derrick Minnie previously of Kohler, Glyn Taylor of C.G. Smith Sugar, Mike Sander of AECI and Spencer Sterling of Samcor. They have refocused on cash flow and cash generating capability, in the form of a cash management ethic, in order to determine the value creating performance of their businesses. The point is that head offices in new generation organisations are viewed as the strategic pathfinders and bankers for the larger organisation. They are used as and when required, and compensated at market related financial rates — hence the rent-a-head-office concept — leading to a major shift in focus from being fund-absorbing (cost centre) to becoming self-funding.

Renewing management activities

The need to overhaul the entire work process of the organisation by removing work that does not create customer value has been enhanced by concepts such as the value-chain, and the collapse of the vertical organisation in favour of its horizontal counterpart. South African managers are finding it increasingly difficult to cope with the tempo of change demanded by these new trends. Causing a seismic shift in organisational thinking is not part of the natural fabric of South African management's style.

The key discovery among new generation organisations is that organisational change is a function of the way managers change the way they perform their day-to-day work in managing the organisation. Large numbers of managers indicated that it is wishful thinking to expect fundamental changes in the mindset of employees and divisions, if this is not preceded by revolutionising management practices among the key people in the organisation. New generation organisations simply believe that the future role of the manager is one where every activity performed on a day-to-day basis must add direct value to those that interface with the customer. If the work that managers perform does not meet this test, then it needs to be changed or eliminated. Dealing with the entrenched reports, approvals, meetings and procedures (known as *RAMP's*) is fundamental to implementing this procedure. The cages need to be rattled continuously. This principle is applied successfully in organisations such as ISG, Dulux, Times Media, ABI, Langeberg Foods, SAA, Metropolitan Life, Sentrachem, Ampros, Dorbyl, Afrox and Telkor. In all these organisations there is a continuous shift in managements' responsibilities — the only consideration being the ultimate efficiency of corporate performance.

In renewing management activities, new generation organisations categorise themselves in several ways:

- Core activities that can only be performed by the manager, because they create value for the customer, and directly add value to those business areas that serve the customer.

- Core activities that should more appropriately be performed by subordinates, because direct involvement by the manager would not be cost-effective and would slow down decision-making.

- Non-core activities that do not create value for the customer, or add value to those business areas that serve the customer base. These activities should be conducted elsewhere, or stopped immediately, even if already agreed to in the current budget.

- Non-core activities that do not significantly enhance the core competence of the organisation, and which could more appropriately be outsourced. This would shift the fixed cost base of these activities towards a variable cost base.

New generation organisations report that this process causes substantial friction, ensures widespread creative tension and guarantees extensive demolition of old paradigms about value-added management activities.

There are several techniques which can be used in driving the process of moving down, moving out, or halting non-value creating management activities. (See Figure 8.)

Moving down

The issue of empowerment through the delegation of management activities is a very contentious one. It requires that every conceivable activity in the day-to-day schedule of the entire management superstructure is intensively reviewed.

Figure 8. Overhauling the work format in the value-chain

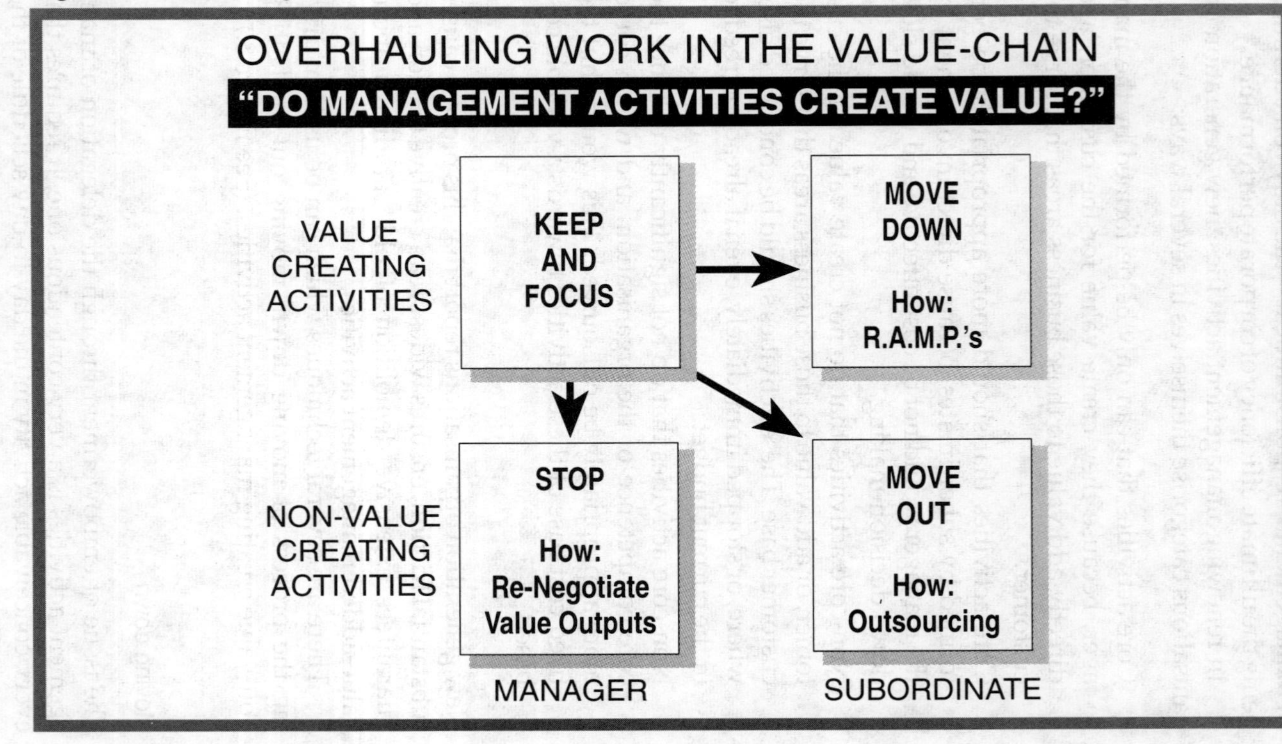

The aim is to remove from management any decision activity — RAMP's (report, approval, meeting, procedure) — that could more appropriately be performed by the subordinate structure, without a substantial increase in the probability of errors of judgement to the organisation. The acid test according to Bruno Penzhorn of Rotek is that if any activity, because of a lack of authority, unnecessarily slows down the decision-making of the operating levels, this activity should be delegated elsewhere within the organisation. The research found numerous instances where middle managers believed that they lacked the authority necessary for their levels of responsibility. They felt that they required a higher level of discretion.

The most obvious areas typically included unnecessary head office questions (paperwork, reports), long-winded memo's, thick documents, convoluted plans, long meetings, strict head office approval limits, time-consuming authorisation procedures, long review cycles, complicated policies, overly prescriptive procedures and rigid job prescriptions. Participants in the research reported that up to 35% of the daily management activities listed above could be delegated without affecting the value-added contribution of management.

Moving out

The budget ownership approach emerging in the head offices of new generation organisations has important implications for the trend towards outsourcing. Non-core value-chain activities are either located outside the business in separate profit centres, or, where internal support areas have been rationalised, these services have been sourced externally.

Outsourcing is still in its infancy in South African organisations. The indications are, however, that given the attractive benefits of moving from a fixed to a variable cost basis for many of the support functions, the approach is gaining considerable momentum.

The key problem appears to be the question: How does the organisation distinguish between core support areas, and non-core areas that should be outsourced? The answer is contained in the value output approach. Any activity which the line managers do not perceive to be of immediate and critical value to the achievement of their priority objectives, should be outsourced. Such activities could be identified via a core competence audit.

Outsourcing decisions are ultimately tied to the concept of budget ownership. Managers can only make sensible business decisions on outsourcing opportunities if they are suitably committed (psychologically contracted) to the achievement of specific budget items. The research indicated that where such a commitment to pinpointing outsourcing opportunities was lacking, managers refused to take the responsibility for the negative consequences. In such organisations managers complained that their subordinates avoided being involved in issues relating to outsourcing.

Move elsewhere, or stop

This approach requires considerable maturity among managers. New generation organisations report that support function managers are easily threatened when activities they consider to be vital, are identified as non-core by line managers who have different views about the immediate priorities facing the business. The best approach in this process is to do a complete review of the service level agreements between the various parties who are involved in the value-chain. Such service level agreements usually reflect the value outputs and expected performance standards agreed between the line and support functions. If the line complains about activities that do not directly add value, then management has a responsibility to review the original service agreements.

When downstream business divisions identify activities they view as non-core, and which they would prefer to move elsewhere or stop completely (temporarily or permanently), because they do not add value, then the existing service level agreements should be re-negotiated.

Integrating diversity through strategic planning

One of the major findings of the research has been that there is a lack of integration in organisations when enhancing the few core strategic capabilities that already exist. This is particularly the case in large, diversified businesses. Several large South African organisations have been publicly criticized for their poor focus on value-added growth (eg. the sum of the parts is perceived to be worth less than the individual businesses). They are perceived to have a *zebra image* in which the core business remains the dominant focus in terms of value-adding, while newly acquired businesses do not receive the same attention. Many South African business leaders caution that strategic planning for building corporate capability should not overrule common sense.

Planning is often viewed in a glamorous context while insufficient attention is paid to the day-to-day issues of making things happen. Furthermore, the mechanistic feature of the strategic planning cycle in many traditional-trend organisations has decreased the opportunity for debating the core issues.

Leading South African turnaround specialists — Derek Keys (currently Minister of Finance, Trade & Industry), Meyer Kahn (S A Breweries) and Grant Thomas (Malbak) — suggest that strategic planning in South Africa is in danger of becoming a paperchase. Kahn claims that corporate planners cause their own demise by focusing on too many projects at a time. He says : "When it comes to how you get there, I will not accept more than two key issues — I prefer one, but I am getting older, so I'm more patient. What we do is to get at the core of what the issues are and to concentrate on doing the right things. And no matter the size of our business, one cannot do more than one major thing well at any one time".

Malbak has similarly maintained a disciplined approach to strategic planning. Former Chairman Derek Keys espoused the belief that corporate management should be measured by their ability to identify one billion Rand project every five years in order to ensure new investment horizons. This trend has been mirrored in large South African utilities such as Transnet and Eskom. Eskom recently took a decisive and bold step by trimming the strategic priority list from over fifteen to only four key objectives. These were then cascaded through the business at a very rapid rate.

An interesting finding of project research has emerged from the application of a simple test of consistency, integration and focus among management in the traditional-trend organisations. General managers were asked to list the three most urgent concerns they believed their organisations should address to achieve their budgets without jeopardising competitiveness. These lists have shown an amazing variety of outcomes with as many as 15 or more urgent issues regularly emerging. A rule of thumb is to have no more than five or six priorities. It is no wonder, therefore, that these organisations suffer from a lack of focus, horizontal integration and poor follow-through on implementation.

The findings, furthermore, indicate that many organisations focus on the wrong benchmarks in assessing business fit, horizontal integration and adaptability. New generation organisations on the other hand, appear to favour a very specific focus on those corporate performance indicators which affect the key value outputs expected by the customer. They seem to spend substantially more time debating and analysing a core set of indicators that together comprise one overall corporate performance index, against which the entire business is measured.

These corporate indices consist of a multi-dimensional set of ratings by all stakeholders on such issues as value-added, costs, speed of delivery, service levels and corporate ethics. The intriguing aspect of this approach is that while each part of the business has a different contribution to make in improving the overall corporate performance index, a regular and incisive debate by management ensures a healthy exchange of ideas and provides more integration than any formal mechanism would achieve.

The quality quandary

The upsurge of the quality crusade which emerged during the 80s has started to come apart at the seams. Many managers in the study pointed to the dangers of becoming too focused on quality and quality re-engineering, at the expense of everything else. Developments in the West German automotive industry provide a good example. The malaise in the performance of organisations such as Daimler-Benz, Volkswagen and Audi are ascribed largely to the fact that their quality obsession has caused widespread quality excesses. Instead of building in "just-enough-quality" the emphasis has been on "more-than-enough-quality". The negative result of this zealousness is functional narrowness which traps the organisation into the traditional mode of doing things.

The consequences have been self-evident. What these organisations have gained in quality, they have lost in competitive agility and rehabilitative speed. Entrenched routinisation of quality methodologies has overtaken enterprise and these organisations are losing their ability to adapt.

The corporate bureaucrats have found a new haven under the banner of scientific quality management. They have either perpetuated or resurrected the corporate chimneys in following quality at any cost. Presently, many South African organisations are also recognising that to build competitive edge on superior quality alone, is a fallacy. Competitors are often able to negate the quality gains of industry leaders by using technology to copy performance and pricing advantages in developing and marketing new products.

Second-wave cultivation

South African organisations underestimate the importance of managing the new succession which will eventually replace the existing key players in the critical value-chain areas of the organisation. The research highlighted gross negligence in large established organisations regarding adequate talent development for ensuring future industry dominance.

Many organisations suffer from a *succession deprivation syndrome* — not having a sufficient depth of new talent to perform understudy duties for senior managers. This leads to a position of overburdening of the present management. Very few pro-active strategies exist for correcting this deficiency.

New generation organisations have replaced the traditional succession planning systems with second-wave cultivation of new talent within the organisation. Organisations such as Engen, Spescom, JCI, CSIR, Transnet, Foschini, Santam, American Swiss, Barlows, Sasol, the SA Post Office and Telkor have used second-wave cultivation in building a pool of new talent within their businesses. The focus in these organisations has shifted away from intricate and complicated succession planning processes which are aimed at steering managerial talent through a specific pathway in the organisation. Instead they have identified employees who are the new generation of opinion and climate creators, and attempt to *mentor* and guide them without necessarily using structured career paths as the baseline. This approach to creating succession for future key positions recognises the reality of personalities and individual styles in making succession decisions. For instance, the personal chemistry between boss and subordinate, or between chairman and chief executive is critical in determining who will be included in the succession cadre.

Project research identified several interesting "rules of the game" in new generation organisations which emphasise the importance of *mentorship* in developing new management talent. These rules clearly avoid the pitfalls encountered during many thousands of mentoring relationships in South African organisations during the 80s. The counter-trend organisations recommend a basic set of guidelines which should govern the development and nurturing of a mentor-protegé relationship:

- **Identifying a mentor.**
  Look for mutual benefits in identifying a mentor. From the outset the participants focus extensively on building a mutually beneficial relationship. In the case of a one-way development focus where the mentor may feel deprived or see little chance of self-development, the relationship appears to be short-lived. These benefits are stated and discussed from the beginning, and regularly revised.

- **Symbolism and setting.**
  Symbolism and setting are critical. Both the spoken and unspoken issues remain equally critical. The symbolic rituals of management (eg. memo's, social interaction during meetings, formal and informal social contact, company events) should be carefully utilised to add to the protegé's development. If either party fails to be consistent in behaviour, the relationship is doomed. In addition, the setting in which the regular discussions between mentor and protegé are held is crucial, and should therefore be carefully selected.

- **Set specific targets.**
  Targets, both personal and business-related, should be set between mentor and protegé. Favourite issues that form the basis of the need for mentoring include coping with a challenging new management position, becoming a change master in dealing with large-scale organisational change, understanding the unwritten ground rules and *social memories* of the organisation, and familiarisation with the specific business technology.

- **Total confidentiality.**
  Participants were adamant that strict confidentiality was paramount for the good of the relationship. Many issues are discussed that may be sacrosanct to the particular

manager. This requires that the relationship upholds the same stringent standards found in any other typical professional relationship (eg. doctor-patient).

- **No surprises.**
  Participants reported that it was critical that both parties be fully informed regarding the issues on the agenda. Nothing irks a mentor more than unwarranted surprises. The same applies to the protegé.

- **Don't assume anything.**
  Too often matters are taken for granted on the basis of some preconceived assumptions on the part of both mentor and protegé. Such assumptions can often lead to problems, particulary if they are not based on reality.

- **Plan and diarise discussions.**
  Successful relationships appear to be conducted in the format of "business-as-normal". All discussions are treated as part of the regular business process, with meetings being diarised and allocated the same priority as other important business events.

- **Structured feedback.**
  Participants should draw up a structured, formal format for providing regular feedback on progress, issues and new concerns. This should provide both an opportunity to review progress and set new objectives.

- **Create a network.**
  Mentors often prefer protegés to develop an extended mentor network in cases where the mentor is not always readily available. Such networks should, however, be in line with with what the mentor is attempting to achieve.

- **Ensure a hot-line.**
  Emergencies do often occur at inopportune moments. During such times the protegé should have access to the mentor for guidance and advice. However, this should

never be abused and specific rules should be clearly discussed beforehand.

A newly emerging pattern is the acknowledgement by new generation organisations that designing career path systems primarily for upward mobility is a dangerous fallacy. Organisations that are paying attention to the concept of mentoring include Edgars, JCI, Anglo American Corporation, Corobrik, Eskom, Malbak, SA Breweries and First National Bank. These organisations recognise that planning for horizontal versatility of key specialists and generalists is as important as ensuring upward mobility for prospective future business leaders. The traditional wisdom of "successful people move upwards" is being critically questioned by counter-trend organisations. In addition plateauing has become a reality, at least in the Western world. It has to be accepted that sideways career moves are unavoidable in the case of organisations that cannot provide further upward mobility. This may be due to such issues as flattening of the structure, stagnation of the business or bottlenecks. *Rightsizing* has further focused managements' attention on the issue of limited vertical mobility. The restricted opportunities for vertical mobility have caused organisations to critically review the diminishing talent pool and the mechanisms for ensuring long-term core competencies within the nucleus of the value-chain.

In addition to the emerging concerns about future succession, counter-trend organisations face the daunting task of deploying sound, balanced affirmative action strategies for rapidly expanding the talent pool within the organisation. Interestingly however, the debate in new generation organisations about a "politically correct" strategy in South Africa, rejects the notion of tokenism, and the type of window-dressing that pervaded South Africa during the 80s. The new approach is one of equalisation of opportunity and is described by such idioms as Portnet's "row-with-us, grow-with-us" philosophy. This suggests the principle of reciprocity of commitment towards development — that the organisation will commit itself to those employees who in turn commit themselves to the organisation. This acknowledges the interdependence between management and employees in creating equal opportunities for development — it must be a win-win situation.

CHAPTER SIX

Energising the people

Competitive energy is defined as the willpower to dominate in an organisation and is a function of its psychological make-up. New generation organisations exhibit levels of competitive energy that transcend the internal deficiencies within the organisation as well as the day-to-day turbulence in the environment. They approach competitive challenges by building and deploying the intangible reservoir of nervous energy inherent within the organisation.

This chapter describes how new generation organisations use competitive energy to ensure that their people have long-term stamina recognising that traditional-trend competitors inevitably perish from mindset fatigue.

PRINCIPLES FOR ENERGISING THE PEOPLE

There are three fundamental principles underlying the energising of the organisation. These are:

- Nuture *competitive angst*;
- Inspire with pack leadership; and
- Manage through *creative tension*.

Principle 8: Nurture competitive angst

Clive Weil, former Chief Executive of Game, coined the concept of *competitive angst* to describe the way he worries about competition. It is a very apt description for the mindset the research team identified among new generation managers. The sense of vigilance, combined with a healthy respect for the unpredictability of the competition, creates an aura which resembles the fear of the hunted, the wariness of the warrior and the fighting spirit of the underdog. Competitive angst typifies the way successful managers run "can do" organisations, despite adversity.

Project research uncovered several organisations that display different forms of competitive angst. The familiar Afrox "twitch" — sitting on the edge of the chair, walking on the balls of one's feet — is also reflected in organisations such as Liberty Life, the CSIR and the SBDC, while the characteristic "hunch" of the SA Breweries group — sniffing out new undiscovered angles on the competition and the marketplace — is reflected by organisations such as Southern Sun, Corobrik, ISG, Langeberg, Barlows Equipment, Times Media and Ampros.

During his time with both the Checkers and Game Groups, Weil was very successful in cultivating a sense of competitive angst among management. This angst is displayed in the form of a relentless drive to improve the edge over competitors. They were never satisfied that the previous efforts were sufficient, and were constantly aware that the complacent leader is the one who eventually "gets the arrow in his back".

Raymond Ackerman of Pick 'n Pay, as well as Grant Thomas of Malbak, Terry Rosenberg of McCarthy Retail, Paul Kruger of Sasol, Anton Moolman of Transnet, Rob Angel of Engen, and Eric Ellerine of Ellerines all held strong views on why organisations that ride the crest of the wave at one stage, fail to sustain their level of competitive advantage. Their views are that brimming self-confidence, large corporate egos and self-indulgence with regard to previous successes, are not part of the profile of a new generation organisation. Weil suggests that businesses go awry when top managers, cursed with their own intelligence, start to "play" on the periphery of the business, and eventually become snared by issues not pertinent to the core business.

According to David Brink of Murray & Roberts and Tony Traher of Mondi, executives who face a turnaround are

well-advised to bring in outside assistance. Existing management often fails to raise the organisational temperature to
the required level of angst because they have become
prisoners of their own experience. While the conventional
truism holds that external people will miss the important
cues at the initial stages, Weil believes that "what this person
loses on the swings, he makes up on the roundabouts. However, this assumes the outsider is an experienced and sea-
soned campaigner."

New generation organisations are particularly effective
in deploying competitive angst for creating a compulsion for
overcoming obstacles in order to win, irrespective of the
odds. New generation managers never say die. They believe
implictly in the probability of winning against the odds —
including their battles with the big gorilla — of seizing the
initiative in the face of adversity and never admitting defeat.
An example of this competitive spirit was recounted by Tom
Eccles of Afcol. Faced with undeniably worsening circumstances in the furniture industry a senior manager was commissioned to search internationally for export opportunities.
Returning empty-handed, the manager was confronted with
a simple choice: do not return without an order — find one,
never give up. After the second trip he was confronted with
the same management demand. Three trips later he had
located a lucrative export opportunity for the Afcol group in
Europe. The formula was very simple: "keep on travelling
until you locate the opportunity. Never give up until you
have met the challenge".

Similarly, Freegold was faced with the exceptional challenge of decreasing its cost base by more than 25%, mainly
due to a collapse in the gold price. It had to cause major
mindshifts in its management or otherwise face the immi-
nent demise of 110 000 jobs in Welkom. Ken Dicks re-
sponded with legendary determination to achieve what was
considered the impossible in the gold mining industry.
Dicks was faced with several factors: an indifferent labour
force, due largely to adversarial management-union relationships; stagnant efficiencies in production technology;

and an already trimmed-down infrastructure due to the rationalisation process of recent years. Against the odds, Dicks with his unique approach to management by collaboration, mobilised the energy of the entire workforce to achieve the impossible. Freegold is now regarded as a benchmark for efficiency in the industry.

An excellent example among professional firms of a leader endowed with the restlessness and fervour born of competitive angst is Bill Carter, Managing Director of Taljaart-Carter, a leading architectural firm. Carter brings a strong sense of purpose, humility and empathy to his firm. He distinguishes between *rock logic* and *water logic*, emphasising the need to "go with the flow" of industry forces and harness their undercurrents to one's advantage, instead of approaching seemingly impossible obstacles with a prior admission of inevitable failure.

Principle 9: Inspire with pack leadership

Real participative management among South African executives is a rarity, particularly in the classical sense of the word. Interestingly, the research has identified a hybrid style which seems fairly characteristic among the majority of South African organisations. It can best be described as a mixture between benevolent dictatorship, cultivated autocracy — many of the top new generation organisation executives can be described as *cultivated autocrats* — and *shuttle collaboration*. While not perceived to be a role model for future leadership, it is apparent that this almost unique South African style has emerged as a result of our special business and political circumstances.

This style is labelled pack leadership. It is characterised by:

- Focusing on the power of the team, as opposed to individual excellence;
- Animal-like magnetism in pursuading followers to move in a particular direction;

- A forceful, charismatic and dominating personality;
- Nurturing important and well-liked team members;
- The ability to understand and use to own advantage the knowledge of the human psyche, especially in the context of team dynamics;
- The ability to use both verbal and non-verbal cues to wield influence;
- The intuitive ability to gauge and enhance energy levels of employees; and
- The utilisation of a "divide-and-rule" approach to great effect when dealing with dissention.

This leader is particularly effective in allowing opposite viewpoints and encouraging strong contenders to emerge from the pack. Counter-trend ideas are exploited to create new perspectives, while weak team members are often marginalised, thereby leading to diminished roles. Divisive employee behaviour such as challenges to the leadership, or threatening the group fabric are dealt with quickly, decisively and with toughness.

Pack Leaders such as Barry Swart of First National Bank, Hennie Diedericks of SA Post Office, Raymond Ackerman of Pick 'n Pay, Glynn Taylor of C.G. Smith, Donny Gordon of Liberty Life, Bert Wessels of Toyota, George Beeton of Edgars, Myer Kahn of SAB, Derrick Minnie previously of Kohler, Mike Myburgh of SAA, Ken Dicks of Freegold, Robert Herbertson of Samcor (Amic), and Whitey Basson of Shoprite-Checkers believe that teamwork is everything and that this type of leadership is an important denominator in distinguishing "can do" organisations from the rest.

Pack leaders create powerful and effective teams. They generate new wave strategies with which they empower their teams to cause pendulum swings in the mindsets of management and employees. Whereas most industry competitors share the same access to resources — capital, raw materials, labour and markets — the difference in the outcome is determined by the quality of teamwork. Says Clive

Weil: "In the end, it is your team against theirs — the rest is detail".

These leaders often use psychological experiences and symbolic events to establish commitment and initiate action. An excellent example is the way that Hymie Sybul of McCarthy Retail introduced the *lapa* and *hanna-hanna* formats into Savells for the purpose of creating a unique spiritual experience among employees. This is done by combining singing, dancing and praying with discussions of organisational progress, workplace problems and business targets.

Principle 10: Manage through creative tension

The essence of an enquiring mind is the ability to ask the right questions about the fundamentals of the business. Insight is enormously helpful in destroying old conventions about the way the employee performs in the organisation, or about the assumptions that drive strategy.

The importance of creative conflict in contributing to framebreaking thinking is, however, often underestimated. Managers with a demonstrated ability to establish new paradigms are known for their ability to thrive on the conflict arising from contending viewpoints. It has been amply demonstrated that whereas in previous years organisations regarded the resolution of internal tensions that arose from the ebb and flow of the management process as imperative, the newest trend is to maintain a constructive level of tension — more commonly known as creative tension. This approach has been described by Pascale as "orchestrating tension ... to harness contending opposites". This process lies at the core of generating new solutions for reshaping a company's competitive focus.

New generation organisations regularly face re-organising or restructuring to cope with environmental demands. These watershed events in the organisational life-cycle depend on the contention between opposite points of view in order to provide the next stage of renewal through an organisational re-synthesis. Ideally, internal differences of opinion ensure a widening of the range of the options available to the organisation by generating different points of view. This in turn provokes new thought processes: disequilibrium may be caused, and under the right conditions, according to Pascale, may lead to self-renewal and adaptation.

New generation organisations encourage contention in both the formal (eg. board reviews) and informal (eg. cross-departmental problem discussions) aspects of the organisation in order to facilitate breakthrough ideas from which contingency plans can be developed. It is thus not unusual for large, diversified organisations such as Transnet, Afrox, Eskom, SA Breweries and JCI, as well as technologically advanced organisations such as Sasol, First National Bank, TML and ISG to actively favour contention management with the specific purpose of replacing old paradigms with new thinking. While the heat generated by this approach is not always well-received by managers who have grown up in typical traditional-trend organisations, project research has identified an acknowledgement among South African companies of the vast benefits to be derived from adopting this approach.

In some instances, contention in the informal organisation is generated by the appointment of strong individuals, with widely different personalities, to the inner core of the company. It has become commonplace in many organisations seeking new wave and visionary strategies to appoint outside executives. These individuals generally contribute very different perspectives to the strategic debate and cultivate an enquiring culture within their organisations. Formal aspects of *contention management* are identified when different managers are, often unbeknown to one another, seemingly involved in the same project or strategic action. Simultaneously the situation remains shrouded in ambiguity and uncertainty regarding approval levels and scope of authority. The research team has identified several executives who have a penchant for the contention management style. These include people like Dr John Maree of Eskom,

Desmond Smith of Sanlam, Dr John Job of Sentrachem, Paul Kruger of Sasol, Charles Anderson and Abel Erasmus of the Pretoria City Council, Ray Brown of Langeberg, Dave King of Telkor, Tony Farah of Spescom, Dirk Jacobs of Foodcorp and Spencer Stirling of Samcor.

These executives have led the movement within their organisations to provide a new competitive context as the departure point for facing the radically new direction of their respective businesses. Their common quest was for replacing the conventional paradigms with a quantum leap in their organisations.

Sentrachem for instance, opened up major new investment opportunities in the chemical business at a time when the organisation was facing stagnation due to a lack of direction. In the case of Samcor the executive faced the unenviable task of meshing the Japanese and American cultures into automotive manufacturing (Mazda and Ford), while collapsing four companies into one large conglomerate via a merger. Sasol has faced substantial logistical and market challenges in its controversial history of becoming the petro-chemical giant in Southern Africa. Eskom has been at the forefront of commercialisation, creating massive new electrification infrastructures across Africa, and of facing huge financial and efficiency challenges at the same time.

KEY CONSIDERATIONS IN ENERGISING PEOPLE

New generation organisations reflect a number of paramount issues that face management in building the psychological stamina for the long haul. These issues address energising factors such as mindset, the corporate persona, and empowerment through values.

Mindset for problem-solving

The aim of developing mental toughness in an organisation is to achieve whatever primary objectives it may set for itself at a time when self-doubt, a major setback, or a market crisis threaten to destroy the very fabric of the organisation. An enormous amount of money and energy have been poured into change initiatives in South Africa during the 80s in order to create goodwill and enthusiasm during periods of transformation. The outcome has, however, often been employee indifference and disillusionment due to frustrations encountered in the basic fabric of the organisation's make-up.

The difference in new generation organisations is that they are able to turn their organisations from a slog-mode to one which becomes extremely light-on-the-feet. Such organisations follow a three-phase sequence. They get their people to adopt the basic ethos of "I **may** change things; "I **can** change things"; and "I **must** change things".

The first phase encourages employees to actually talk about the need to change things, without the fear of making career-limiting statements. It means acknowledging that enquiry about the status quo is not only acceptable, but in fact desirable. The major management challenge is to get people willing to speak out, to be heard and to exchange ideas about removing the blind-spots of old paradigms. New generation organisations find that creating opportunities for temporary *vertical job rotation* between senior management and the grassroots greatly assists the process. In certain cases, a temporary rotation of executives in peer positions is also very effective in creating open communication. SAA is a good example of how this approach operates. Mike Myburgh and his executives spent several weeks "walking the floor", covering every segment of the value-chain, in preparing himself for the chief executive's role and creating a turnaround situation for SAA.

The second phase is aimed at giving people the competence to identify problems, as well as an understanding of the management processes and business mechanics required for implementing relevant solutions. The focus is on creating self-managing teams — a movement away from the typical corporate boxes — towards achieving the vision of the business. A particularly effective technique to speed up the learning process is to use best practices transfer forums, in which employees from across the organisation exchange new ideas on how to solve old problems. Organisations which have become change masters in introducing this process are the CSIR, the SA Reserve Bank, Trans-Natal, Pick 'n Pay and the Rotek Group.

The third phase is when people are compelled to transform the way the organisation functions. The main objectives are to reinforce the "new generation" behaviour among management and employees. This phase requires substantial support via the reward and recognition systems. An innovative development is the use of a fairly rudimentary recognition system where people are awarded points for identifying customer problems and eliminating these in the shortest possible time. Internal and external customers are involved in judging the effectiveness of the solutions. The system is not centrally controlled, but rather, each value output area in the counter-trend organisation is encouraged to adapt this approach to its own business area for maximum impact. Organisations which have used a variety of versions of this approach in a limited way are SA Nylon Spinners, Boart International, Dulux, Penta-Marine, the Southern Sun Group, Blue Circle and Telkom.

House-of-cards

Counter-trend organisations have recognised that the maintenance of an organisational mindset through traditional methods of enforcement is somewhat similar to keeping a house-of-cards erect. Creating and sustaining a mindset is an intangible process. The organisational mindset can be visualised as a hierarchy of psychological contracts, starting with the interface between corporate and business unit managers, and cascading through the organisation resulting in a strong bonding at the interface between supervisors and workers. It is literally a constellation of relationships between each respective level of management and their subordinates. What is required is a mutual commitment to a common goal to achieve the business objectives.

Building and sustaining the organisational mindset requires a constant ebb and flow of positive moods, perceptions and feelings about self-image and competitive aspirations throughout the organisation. New generation organisations recognize that the mindset in the boardroom will eventually have a domino effect on the emotional fabric at grassroots. To ignore this reality is a dangerous fallacy. The conclusion is that executives have an enormous responsibility to set the emotional tone across the various organisational boundaries. CEO's are as responsible for the mood on the shopfloor as they are for the mood in the boardroom. They cannot escape or abdicate this responsibility.

The development of mindset

Creating the *corporate mindset* is an organic process. It is common knowledge in new generation organisations that the creation of the mood and message surrounding the mindset needs the involvement of senior management, particularly the CEO, in driving the process. In fact, several organisations reported that the need for regular CEO involvement necessitated a restructure of senior management responsibilities in order to make it possible for the CEO and his executives to be visible at the coalface.

Innovative techniques include CEO debating forums, and corporate breakfasts with a combination of stakeholders. This allows the senior executive direct contact with what is happening on the shopfloor, and in the perception of the stakeholder. Another innovation appears to be visits by cross-functional benchmarking teams within the organisation to other institutions who have been selected as leading role-models of the new generation thinking. These teams are then asked to capture their experiences on video recordings and in reports. They set up debriefing groups, and then lead the value-chain task forces in the organisation towards overhauling the business and introducing the newly acquired information on best practices and processes as quickly as possible.

Corporate persona

The *corporate persona* is made up of a composite set of factors such as the personal values and beliefs of the founders, public profile of the organisation, dress code, and a host of other factors. The concept of the corporate persona is a critical focus point in generating a new mindset within the organisation. It goes without saying that overhauling the existing corporate persona starts with the CEO and his senior management. The expectations they generate in terms of behaviour within the organisation, are cascaded throughout the system. Probably one of the best examples in the retailing sector is the way Raymond Ackerman's competitive zeal has inspired an enduring corporate persona among his troops. For instance, it is well known that irrespective of his personal wealth and accomplishments, Ackerman still worries when the competition lowers the price of bread.

New generation organisations have recognised the importance of the symbolism surrounding the corporate persona. They attempt to use imaging in order to ensure optimum utilisation of available opportunities. Anglo American Corporation for many years focused its imagery around the person of Mr Harry Oppenheimer. Similarly, Rembrandt and everything that it stands for is synonomous with the persona of Dr Anton Rupert. Similarly the entire Liberty Life phenomenon is directly linked to the profile of Donny Gordon. The direct effect of such high profile executives must never be underestimated both in terms of their impact within the organisation as well as the profile to the outside.

Stakeholders

In order to create a new generation mindset it needs to be recognised that the involvement of all stakeholders is necessary to change attitudes and create the pace required to ensure success. The research has shown that new generation organisations go to great lengths to encourage stakeholders

— customers, distributors, suppliers, shareholders, employees and their families — to get involved in changing corporate mindsets. A favourite technique is setting up "neutral" forums in which employees and managers are asked to brief stakeholders about any number of critical issues. This approach invariably elicits a new sense of responsiveness from employees and is particularly relevant when dealing with change in the organisation.

Adding power to the values

A pre-requisite for effective mindset development is ensuring that the organisational values make it possible for the employees to change the way the organisation functions. This provides a powerful lever for management to challenge employees to get involved in creating change within the organisation. Once the process has been started, it cannot be reversed. To quote an old maxim: "If you have taught the bear to dance, you don't stop dancing until the bear wants to stop dancing".

A revealing discovery in project research has been the extent to which organisations have gone beyond the traditional value system in transforming business behaviour. Many organisations are now, for instance, nurturing a climate in which values are debated, interpreted and, where necessary, changed in order to meet the challenges of the future. This has seen the emergence of a new approach called the corporate ideology. (See Figure 9.)

Prof Ian C. MacMillan, who coined the term *corporate ideology*, suggests that bureaucratic strangulation, inherent in most established companies, requires urgent attention in order to sustain a renewal process. Middle management are especially hamstrung by layer upon layer of internal regulations, checks and warnings which require their decisions to be ratified by burgeoning hierarchies of staff specialists. This only slows managers' response times, destroys their initiative and demotivates those who have any aggressiveness at all. Clearly, for a company's middle managers to build and

Figure 9. Building coporate ideology

BUILDING CORPORATE IDEOLOGY

WHAT DOES IT SPECIFY?

- Scope of present and future products and markets

- Drivers for critical functions

- Style of management

- Business ethics

- Attitude to risk-taking

- Attitude to competition

- Attitude to customers and channels

- Attitude to employees

- Attitude to external groups

- Self-image about destiny

UNDERLYING PHILOSOPHY

Once key principles are internalised, the
autonomous decisions made in response to
competitive / environmental challenges will
reflect desired mission-supportive behaviour.

maintain momentum they need to be able to act autono-
mously and confidently under conditions of organisational
change, yet at the same time act in ways that are appropriate
for the overall company they represent.

In trying to distinguish between those companies that
have succumbed to bureaucratic strangulation and those
that, despite increased external constraints, have somehow
maintained their aggressiveness and competitiveness, it appears that an important distinguishing feature is the
presence or absence of a strong corporate ideology. This is a
set of fundamental beliefs held by company members about
how the company and its members should behave in rela-
tion to one another and to the outside world. Somehow, the
more dynamic and aggressive companies are able to generate and sustain a powerful, commonly held set of fundamental beliefs that shape the decisions and guide the behaviour
of company management and employees. People inside the
organisation are aware of this corporate ideology as well as
the priorities and trade-offs that must be made as a result of
it. Management is able to delegate decision-making downwards, secure that subordinates will make decisions that are
"right" and "appropriate" to the corporate ideology, and only
in cases when there are conflicts concerning ideological commitments, or when intense pressures develop to reshape
ideological commitments, do subordinates need to have the
decisions made by higher levels of management.

The challenge in dusting off the well-worn company
value statements displayed on head office walls is to create
a corporate ideology simple enough for everyone to know
"what the rules are" and when they are moving into grey
areas. New generation organisations have realised that, in
most cases, this ideology is implicit rather than explicit.
Therefore thay have done much to make the corporate ideology explicit. (See Figure 10.)

It is an interesting exercise for the chief executive of an
organisation to thrash out, with the senior management of
the company, the equivalent of the "ten commandments" for

Figure 10. Corporate ideology of an international importer-exporter

IDEOLOGY OF INTERNATIONAL IMPORTER – EXPORTER

1 SELL BEFORE YOU BUY

2 WE KNOW MARKETS WE SERVE

3 YOU GET 1 EARTHQUAKE

4 A .45 BEATS 4 ACES

5 SHARKS DON'T EAT PILOT FISH

6 A HANDSHAKE IS A CONTRACT

7 THE BOSS IS BUSY SO BE THE BOSS

8 FIXED COSTS ARE NIXED COSTS

9 SHARE PROFITS, DON'T HOARD PERKS

10 USE THE NETWORK, DON'T HOLD CARDS

their company, irrespective of the official (but neglected) set of company values.

An example of the "ten commandments" of a major South African business (slightly disguised to retain anonymity) appears in Figure 11. The CEO responsible for this organisation would have to feel comfortable that, once issued, these guidelines would provide sufficient direction for the decisions of his subordinates, even if the CEO were *in absentia* for a long time. The challenge in reducing the list to a limited set of guidelines forces the CEO to explain the most fundamental trade-offs he/she expects the subordinates to make. As a validity test, the CEO can also be asked to review with his/her senior management the most important decisions made in the last five years and see whether the guidelines provided would produce the same decisions (where the decisions were "correct"). This can lead to further refinement of the list. This process does much to capture the true ideology of a company.

Several new generation organisations have become good at using the corporate ideology to create simplified value rating systems against which employees evaluate themselves, their teams, managers and departments against particular business conduct standards. These scores are then used to make decisions about promotions, incentives, awards, rewards, new appointments and career paths. This process forms the basis for removing the boss from the value-chain by developing self-discipline among teams. The company then uses the same approach to rate other teams and departments, and provides regular feedback on progress or areas of concern. The most important contribution from the corporate ideology approach has been that, once these commandments or beliefs have been internalised, management are able to use these, instead of the traditional procedures and controls, to discipline people.

In addition, new generation organisations are using imaginative means of smoothing the transitional period in initiating an organisational renewal process. For instance, the management sets up a central body of "ombudspeople".

Figure 11. Ideology of a maritime business

IDEOLOGY OF A MARITIME IMPORT / EXPORT FACILITY

1 WE ARE THE GATEWAY TO SOUTHERN AFRICA'S PROSPERITY

2 TODAY'S CLIENT PAYS OUR TODAY

3 TOGETHER WE MAKE THE DIFFERENCE

4 YOUR CENTS OF IMAGINATION IS WORTH RANDS OF RESOURCES

5 RISK + REASON = REWARD

6 LESS WASTE, GREATER GAIN

7 OUR BUSINESS IS ANCHORED IN HONESTY AND INTEGRITY

8 WE STAND FOR FAIRNESS AND DIGNITY

9 YOU ARE RESPONSIBLE – SEIZE THE DAY AND GROW

10 WE HAVE NO BERTH FOR SECOND BEST

These are democratically elected employees who are requested to act as the conscience of management in the change process, the custodians of the newly identified values, and the guardians of the interests of the employees as rightful participants in overhauling the organisation.

This body has legitimacy in administering the value rating systems within the organisation, and is used to guide decisions about competency development (using the focus of the values), promotional issues, enhancing incentive schemes, ensuring appropriate disciplinary procedures, developing optional career paths with problem employees, and resolving individual performance problems in the case of chronic under-performance.

CONCLUSION

The preceeding chapters have focused on those ten principles which are core to the new generation thinking reflected in this book. These principles, in combination, will cause a seismic shift in the functioning and performance of the organisation and simultaneously give management the ability to leapfrog industry thinking for optimised results. It leads to a level of competency and competitiveness which has become the hallmark of new generation organisations. Such organisations are able to deal with macro issues such as turbulence and globalisation in a way that would never have been envisaged before.

CHAPTER SEVEN

Creating leadership capability

The challenge to leadership in South Africa is to establish and implement effective strategies which have relevance in these very turbulent times. Leaders need to trust their natural instincts when dealing with the risks and uncertainties associated with a turbulent environment.

The crucial issue facing South African organisations is the optimisation of leadership potential. The purpose is to correctly target both the cognitive and conative potential of the leader for the effective energizing of the organisation. A major fallacy in current thinking is the notion that: "...if I am a good planner, everyone else must be a good planner" or "...if I value time management principles and adhere to them, everyone else must be able to do the same." Training does not change the basic person — you can only be what you are.

There is a diversity of both **cognitive capability** — the mental act or process by which knowledge is gained — and **conative capability** — which predicts how each person strives and what each person will initiate or prevent.

Each person possesses a unique cognitive and conative make-up. This cannot be altered, enhanced or diminished — it is a given. From this flow the personality, the distinctive human temperament, leadership style and creative ability of the individual. Sustained productive performance is a function of identifying and targeting this energy correctly.

Obviously, people can get involved in doing things they would prefer not to do. But forcing oneself to do what does not come naturally, can result in stress and burn-out. Under these conditions sustained performance may not occur.

These conditions also account for the low productivity and lack of fullfilment experienced by so many employees in South African organisations.

THE FOUR COGNITIVE PREFERENCES

The concept "cognitive" refers to the mental act or process by which knowledge is acquired, including perception (how a person acquires information through sensing, intuition and reasoning). The most significant contribution to understanding the cognitive mindset of any single individual has come from the pioneering work of the Swiss psychologist, Karl G. Jung, as well as Myers and Briggs.

Myers and Briggs have identified eight respective preferences that exist within all people. These preferences form four pairs of opposites. Each individual is dominant in one of each of the four pairs:

(E)	Extroversion	versus	(I)	Introversion
(S)	Sensing	versus	(N)	Intuition
(T)	Thinking	versus	(F)	Feeling
(J)	Judging	versus	(P)	Perceiving.

A practical way to understand the function of each pair of preferences is illustrated in Figure 12.

Everyone has four dominant preferences. By combining the energising (E/I) and perceiving (S/N) preferences, four useful orientation types are obtained which provide an understanding of how each executive thinks. The four combinations are:

IS (Introverted-Sensing);
ES (Extroverted-Sensing);
IN (Introverted-Intuition); and
EN (Extroverted-Intuition).

The effects of these four combinations of preferences provide the four types of indicators depicted below:

Figure 12. The Myers-Briggs Type Indicator (MBTI) Model

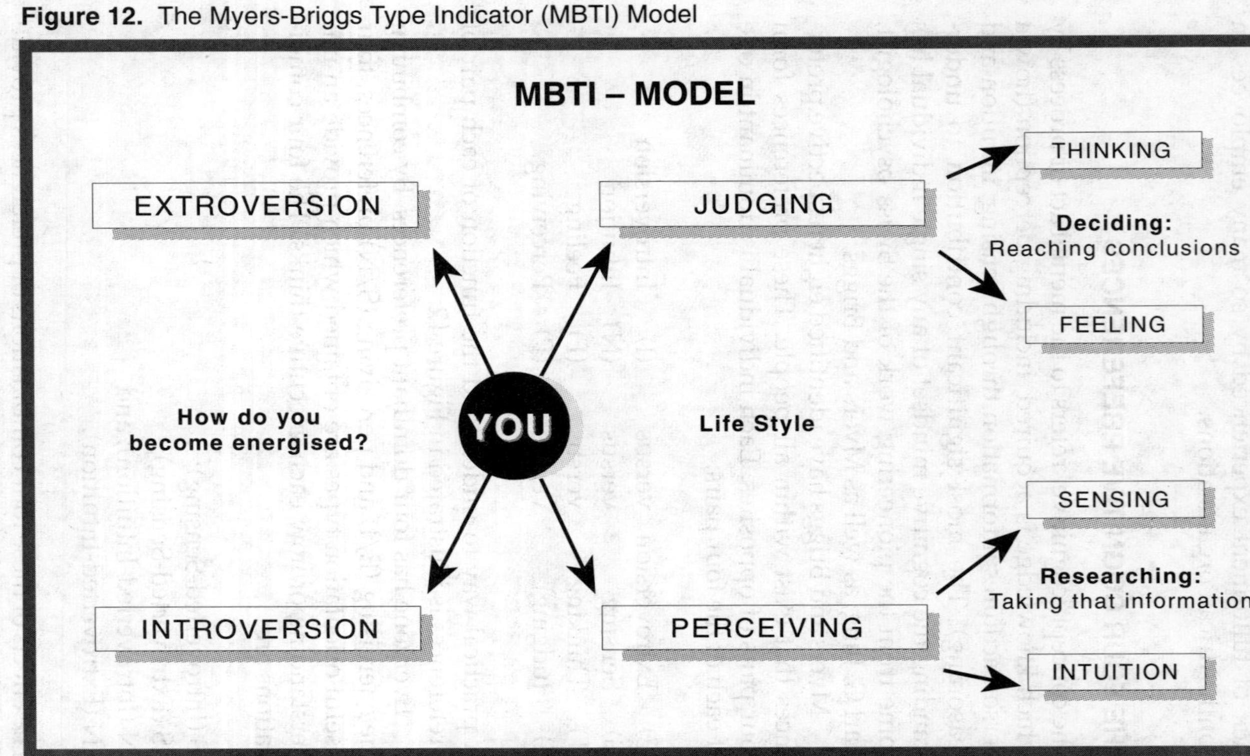

Type 1:
IS (Introverted-Sensing)

	"Let's keep it!"
Individual focus:	Facts and practical considerations.
Leadership:	Lead through ideas. Give attention to what needs doing. Ideas mainly based on the proven. They are thoughtful realists.
Organisational focus:	Continuity of past and present ways of doing things.

Type 2:
ES (Extroverted-Sensing)

	As long as it works "let's keep doing it!" and if new actions are required "adopt what others are doing (the proven thing)".
Individual focus:	Practical action based on the proven facts.
Leadership:	Emphasis is on action and practical, workable solutions. They are action oriented realists.
Organisational focus:	Results oriented.

As can be seen IS and ES executives preoccupy themselves with the present and the past. If they are Judging (J) dominant, they are traditionalists, stabilisers and consolidators. If they have to function as transformational leaders, little change will occur in terms of renewed strategic initiative, because they are not natural change agents. Executives with Perceiving (P) dominance are troubleshooters, negotiators, and fire fighters. Both types, ISJ and ESJ are known for meeting deadlines, while ISP's and ESP's are known for their expeditious handling of the out-of-the-ordinary and the un-expected. Collectively these executives make up between 70-75% of the population. The larger majority are extroverts.

Type 3:
IN (Introverted-Intuitive)

	"Let's think about it differently!" Everything is questioned.
Individual focus:	Intangible thoughts and ideas. Creative thinking for developing theoretical concepts.
Leadership:	Innovative, entrepreneurial, future driven, consider possibilities and take on challenges. They are thoughtful innovators.
Organisational focus:	Visionary, strategically proactive, anticipating or creating change in the midst of opportunity.

Type 4:
EN (Extroverted-Intuitive)

	"Let's change it!". Don't stick to what is not working. Let's make the future happen.
Individual focus:	Architects of systems, builders of relationships, apply new ideas.
Leadership:	They adopt new creative ideas with ingenuity. They are action-oriented innovators.
Organisational focus:	Change-oriented, seize opportunities, focus on possibilities, make the future happen.

As can be seen IN and EN executives preoccupy themselves with forward thinking. Being strategically proactive and future oriented they are the change agents within the organisation. They experience difficulty in communicating and being understood when dealing with their IS and ES counterparts. They have to learn that their frustrations within the organisation often come from dealing with executives and employees who are opposite types. If they do not allow for these different types, they are likely to be misunderstood and become frustrated when change processes are slow. Whenever new solutions and strategies are to be developed and initiated, it is best to put IN's and EN's in charge — particularly if change away from the traditional way of doing things is involved.

Executives with INT and ENT (thinking dominance) work on ideas with ingenuity and logic. They solve problems by using objective analysis of possibilities, moving skillfully from cause to effect. They are adept at developing theoretical concepts and turning these to competitive advantage when they need to act. Executives with INF and ENF (feeling dominance) understand the aspirations of people (employees) and solve problems by adopting a personal view of possibilities. They are good at inspiring others and consider the impact of changes and new initiatives on others.

Collectively, the Intuitives (N) form approximately 25% of the population. Some 70% will be extroverts. Many new generation organisations tend to have leaders who are "N" dominant — this is why they are able to effect a turnaround, achieve organisational culture change and attain a competitive edge over their traditional-trend counterparts. Where new generation organisations have "S" dominant leaders, they tend to be industry/organisation specific. They achieve new generation organisational status because these leaders have appointed a number of "N" executives, who lead with the required style and are usually type 3 and 4.

THE CONATIVE ACTION MODES

Conation is the aspect of one's mental processes that predicts how each person strives and what each person will initiate or prevent.

Kolbe identified four **Action Modes**, the strength of which can be measured. The four action modes are Fact Finder (FF), Follow Thru (FT), Quick Start (QS) and Implementor (IM). The conative creativity for each of the modes is targeted in the following manner.

All four Action Modes are measured on an intensity range of 1-10. Scores of 1-3 in any of the four action modes indicate that the executive is resistant in that mode — i.e. he will not engage in a lot of the actions classified in that particular mode. Moreover, he will prevent others from being too active in that mode.

Initiators (Scores 7-10)

Fact Finder (FF): Conative creativity lies in establishing objectives, defining strategies and assessing priorities.

Follow Thru (FT): Conative creativity lies in formulating systems that provide structure and continuity.

Quick Start (QS): Conative creativity is intuitive, visionary and highly original. The QS has a knack for finding alternatives and discovering unique ways of getting things done.

Implementor (IM): Conative creativity lies in building and developing models, mastering mechanical devices and selecting the right tools and devices for manufacturing and production.

Preventor (Scores of 1-3)

Fact Finders (FF): Avoid getting bogged down by detail, historical data and past events. Avoid offering justifications for past happenings.

Follow Thru (FT): Won't get stuck in routines, won't follow time management procedures. Won't stay with a process or procedure that is not working. Require freedom from prearranged schedules.

Quick Start (QS):   Won't create chaos; won't be rushed; won't go against the odds or take the bait when challenged; won't force change and disruption; need to avoid competitive deadlines. Keep growth from getting out of hand; prevent over-extension of resources.

Implementor (IM):   Won't force tangible solutions, won't require concreteness; don't need to see what is happening at the moment. They push past day-to-day realities towards unseen possibilities.

Kolbe argues that everybody is born equally creative (i.e. everybody has the same four action modes), but not everyone uses their creativity in the same fashion (i.e. the four action modes are manifested by different combinations of strength in each person). Everyone has at least one strong mode and one low mode. In some instances a person may have two strong modes.

Executives will initiate out of their high mode — an insistent mode — when they lead. From the low mode — a resistant mode — executives and employees resist certain behaviours. Where more than one mode is insistent, combinations of conative creativity are formed. The following are examples:

Manager (FF/QS — Insistent):
Conative creativity is displayed by developing strategies, assessing options and allocating resources. (Orientation: "My hunches are right more than 50% of the time.")

Entrepreneur (QS/FF — Insistent):
Conative creativity is displayed by managing innovation and inviting practical alternatives. (Orientation: "I'll bet I can prove them wrong.")

Strategic Planner (FF/FT — Insistent):
Conative creativity is displayed by establishing priorities for carrying out precise and efficient plans. (Orientation: "How does this fit into the system we have?")

Systems Analyst (FT/FF — Insistent):
Conative creativity is displayed by structuring complexities, planning appropriately and charting probabilities. (Orientation: "Everything you'd expect is included.")

Mediator (FF/QS/FT/IM — all 4 modes in accommodative area):
Conative creativity is displayed by bringing about consensus by acting as the unifying force facilitating team efforts. Where an executive has all four action modes in the accommodative range (4-6) or at least 3 in the accommodative range and one resistant, he acts as a Mediator. (Orientation: "Consensus is the best solution for team commitment and performance. People must be empowered".)

SHAPING THE CORPORATE MIND

The organisational **being** is essentially determined by the **corporate mind** — the organisation's energy field which consists of a number of components. First, how we **think** and **perceive** — referred to as the **cognitive dimension** of our human nature. Second, how we **strive** and **perform** — referred to as the **conative will**, which is the basis of pure natural instinct. This energy field sets in motion the beliefs and practices that give life to the web of an organisation's culture, its functioning and direction.

The corporate mind is thus the collective energy field of the cognitive and conative profiles of the leader and his team. Understanding the collective and individual profile of each member of the team, including the leader, provides the insight into how they think, react or proact, and what they will initiate or prevent. If the top team of an organisation is cloned on subordinate behaviour, as may often be the case, this may form a very distinctive basis for the emerging culture of the organisation.

Where cognitive and conative diversity are balanced in a top team, there is a strong likelihood of synergy. This is more than apparent in those new generation organisations which were identified in the project research.

The essential characteristics identified in new generation executives are now discussed.

PROFILE OF THE NEW GENERATION ORGANISATION LEADER

South African organisations are deeply affected by the turmoil of socio-economic and political instability and future uncertainty. Project research has pointed to the increasing difficulty of providing effective leadership under such conditions. For instance, to be able to increase competitive intensity and to transform organisational culture and structure, the research shows that there is a need for visionary Quick Start leadership.

Project research requested eminent business leaders — including Raymond Ackerman, Mike Sander, Clive Weil, Barry Swart, Dr Ben Vosloo, Brand Pretorius, Myer Kahn, Leslie Boyd, Danie du Toit and Dr Brian Clark — to participate in an assessment of the conative action modes of South African executives by using the Kolbe Conative Index (KCI). This instrument identifies four distinctive action modes — Fact Finder, Follow Thru, Quick Start and Implementor. The purpose of this exercise was to determine whether there is a common profile that fits the new generation organisation leader.

The results of the assessment are reflected in the following data:

Fact Finder/Quick Start	Manager	30,4%
Quick Start/Fact Finder	Entrepreneur	13,1%
Quick Start	Innovator	17,4%
Fact Finder	Researcher	17,4%

Fact Finder/Follow Thru   Strategic Planner   8,7%
Follow Thru/Fact Finder   Systems Analyst   4,3%
All Modes Accommodative   Mediator   8,7%

The sample distribution is reflected in Table 1 below. Table 2 reflects the distribution of intensity for all the executives in each of the four action modes.

Table 1 : Distribution of the 4 modes by intensity of action

Mode	Resistant	Acommodative	Insistant
Fact Finder	4,35%	39,15%	56,5%
Follow Thru	30,45%	65,2 %	4,35%
Quick Start	8,7%	47,8 %	43,5%
Implementor	69,55%	30,45%	—

Table 2 : Distribution of the 4 modes by intensity of range

Range	1	2	3	4	5	6	7	8	9	10
FF %	—	—	4,35	4,35	8,7	26,1	34,8	21,7	—	—
FT %	—	4,35	26,1	30,4	26,1	8,7	4,35	—	—	—
QS %	—	4,35	4,35	8,7	13,0	26,1	26,1	17,4	—	—
IM %	—	4,35	65,2	26,1	—	4,35	—	—	—	—

Quick Start Mode

Analysis of Tables 1 and 2 reveals that 69,6% of the leaders in the sample had a Quick Start intensity of 6 or higher. This category is represented by the executives whose respective *modus operandi* (MO's) were categorised as Mediators, Innovators, Entrepreneurs and Managers. The data also revealed that the executives who had a Researcher profile (17,4%) had a Quick Start intensity of 5.

The conative creativity of the Quick Start is visionary, intuitive and highly original. Quick Starts have a knack of finding alternatives, new niches and discovering new ways of getting things done. Quick Starts challenge the way things are done and try to find better and smarter ways of doing them, leading their organisation into new strategic initiatives. Of all the executives in the sample, only 8,7% were resistant in this mode. *The importance of the intensity of this conative creativity in leaders at top executive levels cannot be sufficiently stressed.* This is reflected in Table 3 below.

Table 3: Conative creativity levels — Quick Start

QS Preventors	QS Accommodators	QS Promotors
Resistant Quick Starts won't:	Are willing to:	Will insist on:
be impulsive, create chaos, cause distractions, force change and disruption, or try too many things at once.	go along with risk, participate in experimentation, assist innovation and try alternatives.	acting with a sense of urgency, advancing risk and experimentation.
be rushed or respond to competitive deadlines.	respond to future needs.	thriving on deadlines and future-oriented projects.
	provide challenges and follow other people's hunches.	creating innovation, trying new things and intuitive solutions.
		seeking new niches and making the future happen.
Intensity ranges 1-3 — sample 8,7%	Intensity ranges 4-6 — Sample 47,8%	Intensity ranges 7-10 — Sample 43,5%

The importance of Quick Start conative creativity is stressed, but it must not be taken for granted that every new generation organisation has a CEO or Chairman who is sufficiently dominant in this mode. Where Quick Start intensity was found to be less than 5, the top team of the organisation had at least two or more other top executives with high Quick Start modes.

Fact Finder Mode

Of the leaders in the sample group, 82,6% had a Fact Finder intensity of 6 or higher. The conative creativity of this mode is in establishing objectives, defining strategies and assessing priorities. Clearly these executives provide leadership focus for those they lead by assessing and attending to the most important things first, creating analogies and seeking or providing specificity.

For all executives in the sample only 8,7% were resistant in this mode. Added to the Quick Start mode, specificity, focus, quantifying and rank-ordering priorities are vital aspects of effective leadership in these times of turmoil. Organisations which are not focused lack specificity. The importance of this conative strength is obvious from the information in Table 4.

Table 4: Conative creativity levels — Fact Finder

FF Preventors	FF Accommodators	FF Promotors
Resistant Fact Finders won't:	Are willing to:	Will insist on:
require documentation and a lot of historical facts.	review data and live within the priorities.	quantifying and ranking probabilities and issues.
get bogged down in details or require on-going historical facts.	be specific, go with the highest probabilities.	seeking specificity, collecting data and doing extensive analysis.
over-analyse or require written proof.	review and test analogies and respond appropriately.	defining terms.

FF Preventors	FF Accommodators	FF Promotors
Resistant Fact Finders won't:	Are willing to:	Will insist on:
be tied to tradition.		determining the appropriateness and defining strategies and priorities linked to clear goals.
Intensity ranges 1-3 — Sample 4,35%	Intensity ranges 4-6 — Sample 39,15%	Intensity ranges 7-10 — Sample 56,5%

Follow Thru Mode

The conative creativity of this mode lies in formulating systems and procedures that provide structure and continuity. These persons will seek order, arrange logistics and ensure that things are finalised. They need to act sequentially, integrate the past, present and future, and produce things according to schedule.

Of the executives in the sample 33,45% were resistant in this mode. They require freedom from prearranged schedules, their sense of time is "whatever it takes", and they won't follow time-management procedures.

The conclusion drawn from the results in Table 5 is that a fairly large portion of leaders do not want to be caught up in too many procedures, get stuck with routines, or adhere to a way that is not working. Greater flexibility and less bureaucracy appear to be needed.

Table 5: Conative creativity levels — Follow Thru

FT Preventors	FT Accommodators	FT Promotors
Resistant Follow Thru's won't:	Are willing to:	Will insist on:
require plans or prearranged schedules.	maintain order, stay with the system and follow schedules.	acting sequentially.

FT Preventors	FT Accommodators	FT Promotors
Resistant Follow Thru's won't:	Are willing to:	Will insist on:
stay boxed-in or get caught up in procedures or routines.	adhere to procedures.	organising their time and completing tasks according to schedule.
need consistency or stay with what is not working.	persevere and complete things on time.	seeking order, designing systems, providing charts and arranging logistics.
function by rote or need pictures and graphs.	fill in charts and carry out a certain amount of routine.	focus.
follow time-management procedures.		providing uniformity and working sequentially.
Intensity ranges 1-3 — Sample 33,45%	Intensity ranges 4-6 — Sample 62,20%	Intensity ranges 7-10 — Sample 4,35%

Implementor mode

The conative creativity of this mode lies in the need to create tangible goods. Implementors craft and build prototypes and models. This conative creativity is essential in artisan jobs, manufacturing and wherever sustained skill in working with one's hands is encountered. Of the executives in the sample 95,65% were resistant in this mode. Implementor resistors ignore durability factors, don't deal well with tangibles, lack sensitivity to product quality and do not maintain plant and equipment.

Emerging leadership profile

Substantial variations exist among senior executives in respect of their unique individual profiles. A distinctive leadership profile begins to emerge from the foregoing analysis of the intensity levels of the accommodative to insistant Fact Finder/Quick Start and accommodative to resistant Follow Thru pattern.

What is clearly reflected in the research is that too many South African executives spend an undue amount of time assessing priorities, conducting analyses, establishing objectives and defining strategies. Because insistant Fact Finders also seek specificity, the present levels of environmental turmoil and uncertainty can lead to analysis-paralysis — an over-indulgence in data collection and analysis. Attention should rather be focused on strategic thinking and finding ways which can take the organisation into new niche markets. This, in fact, was found to be the case in organisations such as Rotek, Sasol, Kohler , AECI, McCarthy Retail, Corobrik, Toyota and M-Net.

The new generation organisation leader is essentially recognised as having a strong visionary component in his basic make-up. He is, furthermore, probably entrepreneurial, takes risks, crafts solutions and is willing to experiment. The new generation organisation leader's mindset adopts a before-the-fact posture, thereby making the future happen. He is essentially proactive, positive, and optimistic. He seeks challenges and responds to opportunity quickly. It is estimated that executives with this type of make-up form no more than 22% of the executive population in South Africa.

To deal with the South African situation as well as changing overseas markets effectively, the Quick Start mode is essential for advancing risk, promoting experimentation and ensuring innovative culture change. The majority of new generation organisation leaders, where the Fact Finder/Quick Start modes measured conative intensity levels of 6 and higher, do just that. The new generation organisation leader profile that emerged is one of executives who spend time developing strategies, assessing options, allocating resources, managing innovation, inviting practical alternatives, and demonstrating a knack for finding unique ways of getting things done. These executives are resistant to accommodative in Follow Thru, suggesting that they will not allow themselves to become boxed in or get caught up in unnecessary procedures and routines. They will also not stick to processes or methods that are no longer working. Most of the important Follow Thru tasks are thus delegated for others to attend to.

In addition to the KCI analyses, a further important factor examined by the research is to understand how new generation organisation leaders make decisions. In this study interviews with many of the senior executives made it possible to observe their **Action Profiles**.

THE ACTION PROFILE OF LEADERS

The decision-making process is characterised by three distinct stages namely **attention**, **intention** and **commitment**. Balanced decision-making in management is crucial to an organisation's success. Collectively the three stages reflect six potentials in every human being. Every person's Action Profile reflects the particularly unique pathway their thinking takes as they go through a decision-making process. Executives begin their decision-making process in the areas where they have the highest motivational potential, spending more time and energy in these areas. They then progress through the other areas, depending on the relative magnitude of potential in their profile.

There is nothing good or bad about an executive's particular style of decision-making. However, inherent in everybody's profile are certain strengths and weaknesses. The aim and benefit of being aware of one's decision-making profile is to find ways of working, whether alone or with others, that will ensure that one's strengths are fully functionalised and one's weaknesses complemented. To be an effective decision-maker an executive must **attend**, **intend** and **commit**. Executives will, however, apportion their time and energy according to their preferences.

The Action Profile technique highlights which stages of the decision-making process an executive prefers and whether he/she takes a more assertive or perspective-oriented approach (see Figure 13). Attention-oriented executives define their roles as information gatherers and researchers. Intention-oriented executives will focus on policy-making and difficult projects which test their performance. Commitment oriented executives find ways to put themselves where the action is fast and the competition stiff.

The results obtained from the interviews are provided in Table 6.

Table 6: Action Profile results of business leaders.

	Sample average potential	Intensity of potential		
		> 20%	10-19%	1-9%
Investigating	18%	37,5%	62,5%	—
Attention (Research)				
Exploring	18%	31,25%	68,75%	—
Determining	18%	22,0%	78,0%	—
Intention (Decide)				
Evaluating	14%	6,25%	90,6%	3,15%
Timing	21%	75,0%	25,0%	—
Commitment (Action)				
Anticipating	11%	3,12%	40,63%	56,25%

Potential strengths: 1-9% = Low, 10-19% = Moderate, 20% = High.

Analysis of Table 3 adds additional validity to the conative profile of the new generation organisation leader. In the **attending** stage, the data reveals that the majority of these people are moderate in investigating and exploring, with the

Figure 13: The Action Profile Framework

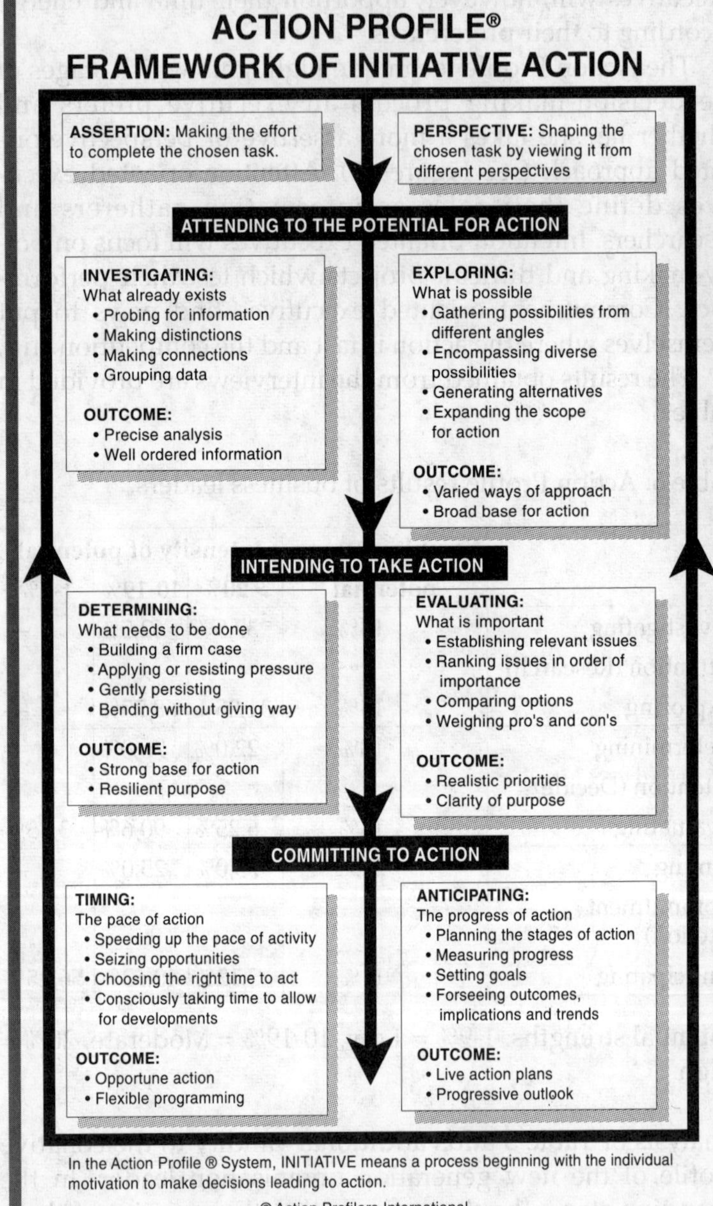

remaining one third being high. Moderate investigators do not want to become overburdened with detail or get caught up in analysis-paralysis. The results for the exploring dimension confirm visionary capacity, the need to expand the scope for action and consider alternative ways of approaching problems. This leads to new initiative and innovation.

The data in the **intending** stage reveals that the CEO's are assertive, persist against odds and maintain a strength of will. They are also flexible in their evaluative style while assessing probabilities, appraising facts and proposals and arriving at a decision. Only a small number had a management style that was somewhat forceful. These executives are likely to receive criticism about their lack of sensitivity and level of aggression.

· In the **committing** stage most of the leaders had very high timing and moderately-low to low anticipation, implying that they have an eye open for opportunities and are ready to act competitively if need be. They are go-getters who get impatient if things move too slowly and may neglect long-term goals and trends in favour of short-term results.

Just as the conative profiles revealed different *modus operandi*, variation also existed among the Action Profiles of these leaders. The results reflect a general decision-making style with variations in each CEO's own profile.

THE IMPORTANCE OF THE TOP TEAM PROFILE

Certain conative profile types emerged as being more general, but it is to be expected that there is no one best or consistent profile that will be the same for each organisation. As products have life cycles, organisations go through a series of evolutionary life cycles.

Periods of growth and transformation require leaders with different conative profiles. When repositioning organisations, identifying new niche markets and going for growth, the major thrust has to be innovation, advancing risk, defying the odds and trying something new. For this process it is best to have leaders who have: insistent Fact Finder/Quick

Start; or Quick Start with accommodative Fact Finder; or Fact Finder with accommodative Quick Start combinations. Evidence of this has been found in the cases of Avis, Edgars, Kohler, SBDC, McCarthy Retail, C.G. Smith Sugar, Pick 'n Pay, Engen, Randcoal, SA Breweries and Toyota. Because most leaders who have the conative creativity for the initial steps of the renewal cycle are accommodatively low to resistant in Follow Thru, it is essential that the top team include two or more members who have the creative capacity to redesign systems, arrange logistics and force closure when necessary. Without this strength the team is likely to initiate more new activities than can be completed in a given time.

Transformation, stabilisation, growth

After a period of rapid expansion or organisational transformation, a degree of stabilisation and consolidation becomes necessary in order to build on past successes. CEO's best at this process are those who have conative profiles with strong Fact Finder/Follow Thru modes. Evidence of this was found in organisations such as SA Breweries, Mondi Paper Company, First National Bank, and in Rotek's case resistant Quick Start. Leaders who are accommodative Quick Starts are uncomfortable with advancing risk and change, but their organisation can undergo transformation and culture change provided that the creative energy of the top team is balanced. Conative diversity presents the opportunity for synergy if these leaders do not become polarised with the strong Quick Starts on their own teams. The formula for success lies in being comfortable with allowing each team member to focus his/her conative creativity correctly. These leaders have to learn to trust the different conative instincts of their team members.

This may not be easy for them, but the organisation's ability to compete, grow and develop a competitive edge in the market is dependent on how the CEO controls the reigns and the degree to which he correctly targets the mental energy of team members.

An example taken from the chemical industry is depicted in Figure 14. The profile is that of the top team of a subsidiary within the group.

Until recently this team provided exclusive specialist services to the entire group. Policy changes within the group now allow other divisions and subsidiaries to outsource these services from competitors. Conversely, this organisation can offer their services to other industries in the open market. Where they previously enjoyed protection within a closed system, they now have to transform their thinking and actions to becoming a major competitor in the open market.

Figure 14 reflects each executive's MBTI and conative profile. The MBTI (personality type) is reflected by four dominant letters, and the conative profile (MO of how each executive strives) by four numbers. The numbers reflect, in order from left to right, the conative intensity of the Fact Finder, Follow Thru, Quick Start and Implementor modes. A score range of 3 or less in any mode implies that the executive is resistant in that mode and will not initiate striving for that particular mode. Where the numerical values range from 4-6 he is accommodative, while scores of 7 or more reveal the areas from which an executive leads and initiates consistent action.

Analysis of the top team reveals the following:

Cognitive Type

IS	ES
"Let's keep it as it is" N = 6	"Let's keep on doing it as long as it works" N = 1
IN	EN
"Let's think about it differently" N = 0	"I like the idea let's change it" N = 2

IS = Introvertive-Sensing / ES = Extrovertive-Sensing

Figure 14: Management team in the chemical industry

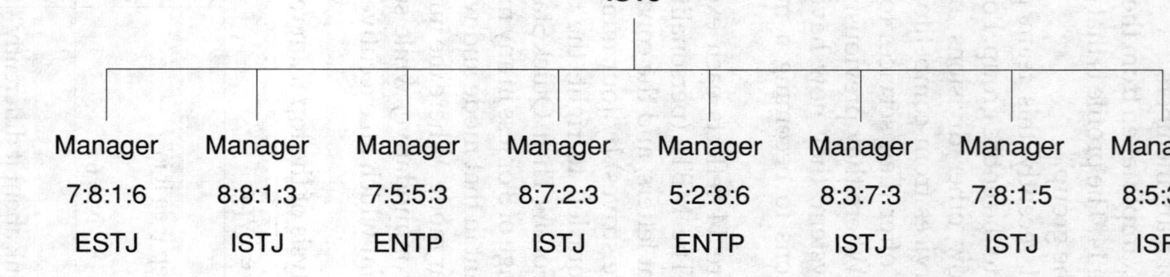

* Numbers reflect the KCI scores for the four Action Modes.

IN = Introvertive-Intuitive/EN = Extrovertive-Intuitive

The team analysis reveals that seven executives display the thinking of traditionalists, while two have the action-orientation of change agents. The six Introvertive-Sensing executives will focus on continuity. They will recognise the pertinent facts, apply experience to problems, notice what needs attention, keep track of the essentials and handle problems with realism. They are likely to see the future in negative terms, can be unduly pessimistic, can get caught in a rut and may not see possible solutions.

The Extrovertive-Sensing executive is likely to be good at analysis, finding flaws in advance, holding consistently to a policy, standing firm against opposition and focusing on practical action and results. He is likely to be hyper-sensitive and take any form of criticism very personally.

The two Extrovertive-Intuitive executives will focus on change, systems and relationships and lead through enthusiasm. They will tackle problems with zest, watch for essentials, recognise new possibilities and supply ingenuity for solving problems. If not counter-balanced by their IS colleagues, they can become obsessed with unimportant details and irrelevant facts.

Cognitively this team is cloned in its thinking. It will have problems achieving a real competitive advantage. The two EN managers will frequently experience a sense of being pushed out, or find themselves in a polarised position with their colleagues.

Conative mode

The conative creativity of each of the executives reveals what they will initiate or prevent. The quantative figures on a score from 5-10 represent in order, reading from left to right, the 4 action modes: Fact Finder (FF), Follow Thru (FT), Quick Start (QS) and Implementor (IM). What each executive will **initiate** (7-10), **accommodate** (4-6) and **prevent** (1-3) can be seen by consulting the scores on Figure 15.

This top team's conative composition is as follows:

FF/FT (5)	Conative creativity lies in establishing priorities for carrying out plans that are precise and efficient.
FF (2)	Conative creativity lies in establishing objectives, defining strategies and assessing priorities.
QS (1)	Conative creativity is intuitive, visionary and highly original. Quick Starts have a knack for finding alternatives and discovering unique ways of getting things done.
FF/QS (1)	Conative creativity lies in developing strategies, assessing options and allocating resources.

If one now examines the team's collective conative intensity across the 4 action modes as depicted in the team synergy chart below, the team's strength is insistent Fact Finder/Follow Thru with more resistant Quick Start. There is also a negative synergy curve revealing that this organisation will have great difficulty developing a proactive, competitive, strategic initiative in the marketplace.

Company X synergy chart

	FF	FT	QS	IM	Synergy	Norm
Resistant	—	2	6	4	12	
		22,2%	66,7%	43,4%	33,3%	25%
Accommo-dative	1	2	1	5	9	
	11,1%	22,2%	11,1%	56,6%	25%	50%
Insistant	8	5	2		15	
	88,9%	55,6%	22,2%	—	41,7%	25%

It can be argued that no organisational renewal process to develop the required cultural change for becoming a dominant market leader can be sustained having this team composition. The single **Innovator** with the KCI profile 5:2:8:6 will be frequently polarised by his colleagues who form a dominant clone. The team will be over-analytical, too procedure bound, and its major source of business will be based on what traditionally works, what is currently adopted and acceptable in most industries world-wide.

Its niche focus in the market should be "expertise input on what experience has taught us, supported by a high degree of efficiency". It can build its reputation on being a reliable organisation that has years of experience and will deliver on time. Efficiency will rank high, but not speed and simplicity. This organisation will not be a trailblazer unless more Quick Start is injected into the top ream with at least two more Intuitors.

Company Y

Company Y is one of a number of organisations within a holding company. The organisation is in the engineering field and a supplier of special maintenance and repair services to the market. The top team comprises nine executives (see Figure 15).

Cognitive Type

IS	ES
"Let's keep it as it is" **N = 0**	"Let's keep on doing it as long as it works" **N = 1**
IN	EN
"Let's think about it differently" **N = 5**	"I like the idea let's change it" **N = 3**

IS = Introvertive-Sensing/ES = Extrovertive-Sensing
IN – Introvertive-Intuitive/EN = Extrovertive-Intuitive

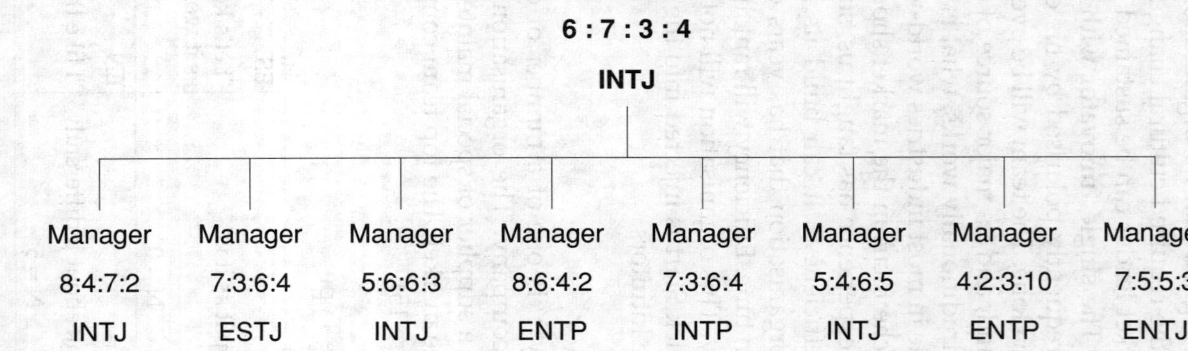

Figure 15: Management team in the engineering field

The majority of the executives are Intuitive-Thinkers with one team member dominant in Sensing-Thinking. This group of executives are therefore focusing their attention on possibilities. More specifically, the mindsets of the five Introvertive-Intuitors (IN's) is to lead through ideas, attending to what needs doing, and supplying vision to the team. The three Extrovertive-Intuitors (EN's) lead through enthusiasm, focus on systems and relationships and like to implement change. The remaining Extrovertive-Sensing executive leads through practical action and focusing on results. Getting things done is more important than a lot of theorising. The team will be acknowledged for its ability to provide strategies as well as analyses of situations, challenges and issues.

While this team has the cognitive make-up to be a trailblazer, it will have problems in that it is too strongly cloned in the Intuitive-mode. This team's potential ability to trailblaze is further supported by its conative profile.

The distribution of the team's conative striving is depicted in the synergy chart below.

Company Y syngergy chart

	FF	FT	QS	IM	Synergy	Norm
Resistant	. —	3 33,3%	1 11,1%	6 66,7%	10 27,8%	25%
Accommodative	4 44,4%	5 55,6%	6 66,7%	3 33,3%	18 50,0%	50%
Insistent	5 55,6%	1 11,1%	2 22,2%	—	8 22,2%	25%

Analysis of the synergy chart reveals that the team has a good synergy curve. There is sufficient conative diversity among the team members to enable the executive team to achieve its objectives. The latter holds true provided the conative fit between each executive and his job is correct. Interpreting the results in the Fact Finder (FF) mode, the team has analytical bias and is inclined to get bogged down in too much detail (analysis-paralysis). A lot of time is being spent on collecting data, establishing priorities, creating analogies, seeking specificity and quantifying issues. The majority of the team is willing to Follow Thru (FT) by maintaining order, following procedures, adhering to the business plan and bringing various tasks to completion. Three of the team members, however, are resistant in the Follow Thru mode, implying that they won't get caught up in procedures, they don't get stuck in routines or allow themselves to get boxed in by bureaucracy. These executives will abandon what isn't working and will need freedom from pre-arranged schedules. They will not be good at following time-management procedures. A problem that exists in this team is that they have too many projects on hand, they set unrealistic deadlines and will have problems completing tasks on time. Unrealistic deadlines mean a lot of pressure on everyone. To compound matters, the team has a great leaning towards Quick Start (QS) implying that they are willing to advance and go along with risk, drive toward the future, identify solutions, experiment and create and support an organisational culture of innovation. The Quick Start insistant infuses an overall sense of urgency into the organisation. For some employees the pace will be too fast.

The prediction that can be made is that this company will be able to ride out the difficult economic times. As the broader environmental transition proceeds, this team will systematically shift the organisation through a transitional phase which will be poised for growth. One can predict that the changes to be made after a period of consolidation will be towards a systematic culture change and restructuring that will allow many more innovations.

CHARACTERISTICS OF NEW GENERATION ORGANISATION LEADERS

In summary, the profiles highlight a number of key characteristics of new generation organisation leaders. They tend to project the following:

- Are fleet-footed;
- Are assertive and tough;
- Apply "light government" with a clear focus;
- Are visionary, intuitive and Quick Starts;
- Are flexible, but do not want to be caught up in excessive routines;
- Spend more time communicating with their employees than operating;
- Clearly define the priorities and the strategy;
- Have a passion for performance towards goal attainment;
- Effectively work in teams and encourage open thinking;
- Command loyalty, trust and respect;
- Use positional power sparingly and influencing power in abundance, thereby allowing others to take charge of their own destinies;
- Are sensitive to organisational culture and know how to reshape the organisation's culture;
- Detest clutter and complexity and prefer speed and simplicity;
- Understand the notion of value-adding;
- Are dynamic and positive in their outlook on life;
- Are exceptionally high on personal energy;
- Spend time thinking at a strategic level, questioning and challenging the thinking of their key executives;
- Do a great deal of framebreaking and trail-blazing work;
- Surround themselves with a team of executives of varying cognitive and conative strengths;
- Anticipate and create change in the midst of opportunity or uncertainty; and
- Perscrvere with great courage.

CONCLUSION

The research emphasises the importance of clearly understanding collective managerial behaviour in any organisation. The task of positioning and steering an organisation successfully through the future remains arduous. The predominant needs in this regard are for on-going restructuring, organisational transformation and challenging long-held paradigms. What is evident in the research is that the organisations facing these challenges will demand leaders that are assertive and tough.

New generation organisation executives provide focus and vision, are by their very nature innovative, will advance calculated risk, promote experimentation and try uncharted territories. They craft unconventional solutions and defy the odds as they drive toward the future. These leaders have positive mindsets, substantial self-confidence and persevere in the face of difficult challenges.

The most common conative profile that emerges is accommodative high to insistant Quick Start with accommodative to insistant Fact Finder combinations. Most of these leaders won't get bogged down by routine or stick to something that does not work. They have an aversion to bureaucracy and are flexible. Where the leaders have the conative profile described above, an Introvertive and Extrovertive-Intuitive mindset (EN/IN) is absolutely essential for success. The challenge is to develop an adequate representation of this orientation in executive teams which are expected to cope with the future — as yet a turbulent and uncertain one.

NEW GENERATION TERMINOLOGY

Amoeba	Term used to describe an organisation as a living organism where the component cells (tasks and jobs) grow, diminish, adapt and shift according to environmental conditions and situational demands.
Analysis-paralysis	Overburdening the management process with escalating levels of analysis, without taking any subsequent meaningful action.
Athletic flexibility	Organisational structure and functioning that permits extraordinary agility of movement.
Benchmarking	Drawing performance comparisons between competitors and peer organisations or sections.
Best practices	Emulating practices, methods, applications, processes, behaviours and strategies of outstanding competitors or divisions.
Big divide (wind-tunnel)	Describes the physical, psychological and cultural divide between key areas, functions, stakeholder areas and management levels encountered in the conventional organisation.
Big gorilla	The feared, loathed, belligerent or respected competitor or industry leader.
Bossless organisation	Where the role of the manager has been transformed from the conventional "plan, organise, control" mode at the apex of the power hierarchy of the organisation, to one of cheerleading, enabling, inspiring and allowing subordinate teams to largely manage themselves.
Cash management ethic	Employees treat their jobs with an acute sense of "what did it cost, and how much money did we make" — cash in, cash out.
Clutter	The disorder created by the myriad job activities, procedural details, implementation instructions and task prescriptions that litter the organisation and distract attention from the things that matter.
Collaborative management	Style of management where leadership firmly exercises its prerogatives in setting the vision and direction for the business. It collaborates with employees only on the implementation of strategy, by challenging them to find the pathway and achieve the objective in the most economical fashion.
Competitive angst	The healthy anxiety truly competitive leaders demonstrate about their industry counterparts, and the way they use this tension to reach new heights of performance.

Competitve shake-out	The elimination of weaker counterparts by strong market leaders.
Competitve design	The architecture (structure, focus, processes, resources) that enables an organisation to compete effectively.
Competitve neglect	When an organisation becomes complacent and ignores the behaviour of competitors in the market.
Cone of uncertainty	The zone around the centre of the organisation where people suffer from confusion and insecurity about policy direction and implementation issues.
Continuous discontent	The attitude that compels the organisation to constantly strive to improve present performance.
Continuous stretch	Persistently striving to achieve ambitious aspirations with limited resources.
Core competencies	The essential skills, know-how, intellectual properties and experience that are the basis for the enduring competitiveness of the organisation.
Corporate anorexia	An organisation that has been slimmed down (downsized) to an unacceptable minimum, thereby becoming deprived of essential infrastructure, resources and depth.
Corporate boxes	The rigidly defined job structures traditional to conventional organisational hierarchy which do not allow for vertical or horizontal movement in decision-making or creative opportunity.
Corporate canvas	The scope presented by the imaginary painting of the leader's vision for the organisation.
Corporate chimney	Destructive effects of the functional hierarchy in a conventional organisation, where common objectives, issues and concerns are neglected due to self-interest of the separate functions/divisions.
Corporate circus	When an organisation is in a state of disorder bordering on the absurd regarding the way management and employees behave. Represents a state of carefree disorderliness and semi-lawlessness.
Corporate cowboys	Managers who display a pioneering spirit which disregards the subtleties of sophisticated corporate life and conventions, and who prefer a problem-solving style.
Corporate ideology	A set of powerful beliefs shared by all employees, which are so effectively internalised to discipline the organisation, that employees can take decisions to resolve day-to-day customer concerns in the absence of the manager.

Corporate malaise — A state of smugness/comfort/complacency with current performance which has serious implications for competitive agility.

Corporate obesity — When an organisation becomes too "fat" in terms of its structure and staff, resulting in the development of a lethargic way of doing things.

Corporate thunderstorm — An occasional emotional outburst from management, generally precipitated by the discovery of a major error of judgement by a subordinate.

Corporate venturing — When organisations branch out into new areas. This implies a risk profile sometimes calculated, sometimes a little less predictable, in terms of impact.

Corporate zoo — An organisational structure along the lines of the animal kingdom where survival of the fittest is the order of the day.

Counter-trend organisation — Organisation which performs in a manner contrary to the norms for its sector or industry.

Creative tension — Creating a state within the organisation where psychological pressure is brought to bear to enhance employee performance and creativity.

Cultivated autocrat — Descriptive term for a manager suffering from an incurably authoritarian style, but whose well-mannered public facade obscures his true toughness (the iron fist in the velvet glove).

Cultural baggage — The legacy of an inherited culture, incompetent employees, unproductive and bureaucratic practices and negative attitudes that inhibit progress.

Customer encounter — The all-important tangible and intangible points of interaction between the customer and the organisation where the perception of the customer is created or affected (positively or negatively).

Customer worth — The net effect of perceived benefits minus the perceived negatives (costs) experienced by customers subsequent to any transaction with a business.

Decision boundaries — The rigid parameters around a job that outline the discretion that can be exercised to get things done.

Decision ownership — Refers to the locus of responsibility pertaining to decisions within organisations.

Deep jobs — Jobs that are empowered and which carry levels of authority commensurate with management's expectations of output.

Ditikale — A Zulu expression meaning "economy under the sun" — allowing everybody an economic opportunity to create a place in the sun.

Discretionary creep	The inevitable erosion of approval power among subordinate levels as the performance of the organisation deteriorates due to environmental factors or internal causes.
Downstream integration	When the organisation focuses on value-adding to a particular function or process which is already in place.
Edgelessness	Refers to the lack of fixed parameters in terms of jobs or areas of responsibility.
Envisioning	Inspiring employees in the organisation to grasp the leader's vision with a sense of excitement, purpose and fulfilment.
Feet through the stove	Taking up the hottest possible position without recognising or considering the risk.
Fiddler	Style of management where the manager constantly interferes in the affairs of his/her subordinates.
Flat jobs	Meaningless, low authority jobs that are highly prescriptive.
Flea taxi	Business unit or division which creates an additional drag on the organisation without any significant value-adding, because it carries non-productive passengers.
Framebreaking	Events, decisions or ideas that defy the accepted wisdom and create a new framework of thinking for the business.
Functional myopia	Refers to the tunnel vision created by an endless exposure to a particular way of doing things without any effort to break out of the conventional wisdom.
Gain sharing	Equally sharing the spoils of the organisation's wealth creating performance among all employees .
Global-local mindset	The organisational ability to exhibit a global framework of thinking while meeting the demands of the local situation.
Hanna-hanna	An expression describing communication between parties to exchange ideas, views and favours.
Helicopter vision	A 360 degree view of the environment and the opportunities.
High ground	A competitive position of superiority.
Head above the parapet	The organisation continuously scans its environment in order to be one step ahead.
Horizontal organisation	The design of organisation which leads to horizontal integration between divisions, functions and people. It is a concious move away from the conventional wisdom of vertical organisations which, in fact, cause separation between divisions and functions.

Indaba	An African expression for a discussion among several parties in order to make decisions or settle differences to mututal benefit.
Industrial melt-down	When a particular industry reaches a point of saturation or over-exposure which causes it to suddenly lose its pole position.
Initiative-seeking climate	Conditions that encourage subordinates to take charge of finding new ways of creating customer value.
Jumbo risks	Very large risks often taken without much premeditated analysis and hence somewhat of a gamble.
Just-in-time training	Training provided as and when the job requires it.
Just-in-time focus	To give attention to issues as and when required thereby avoiding untimely and unproductive paperwork and meetings.
Kamikaze pilots	Managers who, driven by their egos, tend to take high-flying risks without taking cognisance of the full implications to the organisation.
Knife edge	A moment in the life of the organisation where the outcome of a situation which is critical to future events, can stilll go either way.
Kop gallop	Afrikaans term for brainstorming, which literally translated means "taking the brain on a canter".
Lapa	An African shelter where people gather to sing, dance and eat.
Leapfrog (quantum leap)	To achieve a level of performance or make a smart move beyond the immediate reach of competitors, which requires an extraordinary counter-move on their part to establish a new competitive balance.
Learn or leave	Challenge to employees in a steep learning environment (typical of a corporate turnaround situation) to cope with the demands of gaining competence at a fast tempo, or get out.
Light government	Style of rule in an organisation or country which emphasises decentralised management and encourages autonomy — values, practices, procedures and policies.
Light-hand-around-the-throat-management	A style of management that throttles debate, restricts the imagination and discourages the development of alternative viewpoints.
Light on the feet	Organisational ability to move swiftly, respond quickly and act decisively.
Locus of control	Point of control in terms of steering the destiny of the individual or the organisation. Internal locus means

	self-driven; external locus means environmentally driven and influenced by others.
Loyal resistance	The resistance to important new developments, strategies or changes by the old guard of the organisation who prefer to remain loyal to the way things used to be.
Love bubbles	Giving people a nice, warm, fuzzy feeling, without substance, creating promises and expectations which tend to evaporate after a while.
Macho	The bravado displayed in the attitudes and preferences of organisations noted for their arrogant, cocky, daring style.
Managing through	Style of management where the manager seldom takes the formal reporting hierarchy too seriously when confronting issues at subordinate levels.
Mindset	The set of commonly held beliefs within an organisation which drive the organisation in a particular direction. Generated as a result of corporate conditioning.
Mind shift	The (almost audible) gear change by management to adopt a new way of thinking about the fundamentals of the business, when facing a substantially new set of circumstances.
Multi-skilling	Equipping people with multiple skills — often outside the parameters of their traditional jobs — for the purpose of organisational productivity and continuity.
Mumbo-jumbo	Senseless talking, with little action or substance.
New generation organisation	Organisation which is successfully dealing with the future in terms of the changing business and government environment.
Non-stroking culture	Absence of elementary people recognition practices such as incentives, rewards and encouragement found in progressive organisations.
Off-the-wall	Unorthodox or unconventional strategy, action or comment.
Organisational distress	When the organisation finds itself in difficulties due to inappropriate strategies and an inability to cope with change.
Organisational drag	When the organisation gets itself into a slowdown position due to internally inhibitive factors.
Organisational forums	Regular informal meeting arrangements between employees from different work areas, where issues are discussed, views debated, ideas exchanged and value creating performance reviewed. Feedback is

	given about behaviour, measured against the organisational value system.
Outsourcing	Buying in services which are not part of the core business.
Paradigm shift	A major movement in the mindset of the organisation which causes it to change its behaviour and performance dramatically.
Parking lot	A zone in the management process — e.g. meetings, reports, committees — which affords managers an opportunity to use delaying tactics in order to avoid making certain decisions.
Pup with fleas	Insignificant business unit whose history of bad judgement, mistakes, bad luck and present poor performance suggest a zero probability of survival.
Profile players	Visible performers who tend to establish the ground rules for the industry or sector.
Python log	Major customer concerns requiring top management attention which are contained in a standing list regularly scrutinised to ensure swift action.
Quantum leap	A major physical and mental shift in the way the organisation does things. Results in leapfroging the competition.
RAMPs	The essential Reports, Approvals, Meetings, Policies and Procedures used in the management process to change, discipline and direct the organisation.
Rattling the cage	Vigorously challenging the accepted norms, behaviour, assumptions and practices of employees.
Rent-a-head office	The capability of the head office to be self-funding — being used as and when required — and being paid market-related rates for their value-adding.
Re-engineering	To overhaul the entire structure and functioning of the organisation.
Rightsizing	To restructure the organisation appropriately for effective functioning under present or expected environmental conditions.
Robber barons	Managers or employees who have no scruples about enriching themselves at the expense of the customer or the company.
Rubber-hits-the-road	The point at which the organisation has to face the reality of converting strategy into action.
Skunk works	The practice of encouraging exploration zones in the business where employees can feel free to test new ideas and processes without fear of risks.
Snake killing	Eliminating work that does not create value for customers.

Stakeholder co-destiny	Set of interdependent interests affected by the processes and performance in an organisation. Stakeholders include owners, employees, suppliers and customers.
Slipstreaming	Using the forward momentum of the forces of organisational change to bypass obstacles.
Slog mode	The slow pace of progress in a particularly bureaucratic organisation.
Social memories	The historical prejudices about matters of race, sex and creed that condition people's present behaviour.
Strategic call	When the organisation, in an attempt to establish particular ground rules, takes a definitive posture on certain issues affecting its marketplace.
Strategic fling	A short-lived excursion into new ventures, acquisitions or new product developments, which fails to achieve long-term results due to a lack of commitment from leadership.
Strategic schizophrenia	A flaw in the strategic thinking of the business which leads to conflicting strategic actions contrary to the fundamental mission of the business.
Strategic synthesis	When the organisation consciously attends to the horizontal integration of divisions, people and ideas in order to get a synergistic effect.
Submarine syndrome	Burying the collective head of the organisation in the sand in the hope that fears, challenges or concerns will evaporate.
Succession deprivation syndrome	The organisation is starved of good, upcoming talent on which to build its future as a result of poor planning.
Switchboard syndrome	Management style that passes the buck (up or down) while avoiding the responsibility of taking a stand for fear of getting caught in the crossfire between subordinates and senior management.
Tea and coffee issues	The seemingly insignificant problems pointed out by subordinates as being inhibitive factors in ensuring optimum performance.
Theatre of the absurd	An organisational state in which the actors, working in an uncoordinated and unfocused fashion, present an image of chaos and irrationality, resulting in a comedy of errors.
Town hall meetings	The process of public communication used as a medium of causing common vision for the business. Pioneered by Jack Welch at General Electric.

Trading-your-way-out-of-the-corner	Turning the organisation around by giving customers what they want, at value-for-money prices and service levels, with an adequate return for the business.
Transparency	Making management intentions, customer concerns and organisational issues visible to everybody who is affected by them.
Tunnel vision	Focusing on a specific objective or issue, at the expense of other equally important issues, and losing perspective of the larger picture.
Upward creep	When management over-centralises the business resulting in subordinates abdicating their personal responsibility. Decisions are invariably referred upwards.
Value-chain	The sequence of workflow steps required to give customers what they want, and involving all line and support activities, decisions and processes.
Vlam-in-die-gat	Afrikaans expression describing a very high level of urgency and dedication to get the job done.
Wall-to-wall	An approach, method or process which is intended to provide a total solution to a particular problem.
White hot	An exciting, newly emerging industry, drawing immense interest from industry leaders.
Work-out	Process of organisational renewal and competitive transformation originally popularised by General Electric.
Zebra image	A manager or business unit that pretends to be all things to all people, whether the preference is white on black or black on white.
Zero based	Starting a plan, or renewal process from scratch.

PARTICIPATING ORGANISATIONS

A.B.I.	MCCARTHY RETAIL
AECI	METROPOLITAN LIFE
AFCOL	MONDI PAPER CO.
AFROX	M-NET
AMERICAN SWISS	MURRAY & ROBERTS
ANGLO AMERICAN CORP.	PENTA MARINE
AMPROS	PICK 'N PAY
AMIC	PORTNET
AVIS	RANDFONTEIN ESTATES
BARLOW EQUIPMENT CO.	RANDCOAL
BARLOW RAND	ROTEK GROUP
BLUE CIRCLE	RUSTENBURG PLATINUM
BOART INTERNATIONAL	SAA
C.G. SMITH SUGAR	S.A.B.C.
CITY OF DURBAN	S.B.D.C.
CITY COUNCIL OF PRETORIA	SAB — BEER DIVISION
CITY COUNCIL OF SANDTON	SA BREWERIES GROUP
COROBRIK	SA DRUGGISTS
COURT HELICOPTERS	SA NYLON SPINNERS
CSIR	SA POST OFFICE
DEPT. OF FINANCE	SA RESERVE BANK
DEPT. OF TRADE/INDUSTRY	SALES HOUSE
DORBYL	SAMCOR
DULUX	SANLAM
EDGARS STORES	SANTAM
ELLERINES	SASOL
ENGEN	SENTRACHEM
ESKOM	SHOPRITE-CHECKERS
F.N.B.	SOUTHERN SUN GROUP
FOODCORP	SPESCOM ELECTRONICS
FOSCHINI	SPOORNET
FREEGOLD	STANDARD ENGINEERING
I.D.C.	TELKOM
I.S.G.	TELKOR
J.C.I.	TIMES MEDIA LIMITED
JET STORES	TOYOTA SA
J.S.E.	TRANSNET
KOHLER	VIAMAX
LANGEBERG FOODS	WESGRO
LIBERTY LIFE	
LION MATCH CO.	
MALBAK	

ARGENTI, J. 1976. *Corporate Collapse: The Causes and Symptoms*. London: McGraw-Hill.

BARTLETT, C.A. & GHOSHAL, S. 1989. *Managing Across Borders — The Transnational Solution*. Boston, Massachusetts: Harvard.

BENNET, A. 1991. Study says downsizing firms may not bring profitability. *The Wall Street Journal*, Europe, June 7-8, p. 6.

BENNET, A. 1991. More US Chief Executives are being forced out by boards. *The Wall Street Journal*, Europe, June 7-8, p. 6.

BIBEAULT, D.B. 1982. *Corporate Turnaround — How Managers Turn Losers Into Winners*. New York: McGraw-Hill.

BIBEAULT, D.B. 1979. *Corporate Turnaround — Reasons for Decline, Challenges to Management, Strategies and Practices for Renewal*. DBA Research Report, Golden Gate University. Ann Arbor, Michigan: University Microfilms International.

BOLMAN, L.C. & DEAL, T.E. 1991. *Reframing Organizations*. San Francisco: Jossey-Bass.

BUREAU OF FINANCIAL ANALYSIS. 1981. *Financial Ratios and the Prediction of Financial Failure in Industrial Companies in the Republic of South Africa*. Pretoria: University of Pretoria (Report E1).

CAMERON, S.K., SUTTON, R.J. & WHETTEN, R.G. 1988. *Readings in Organisational Decline: Frameworks, Research, and Prescriptions*. Cambridge, Massachusetts: Ballinger.

CLIFFORD, D.K. & CAVANAGH, R.E. 1988. *The Winning Performance*. London: Bantam Books.

CETRON, M. & O'TOOLE, T. 1990. *Encounters with the Future*. New York: McGraw-Hill

CONSULTATIVE BUSINESS MOVEMENT. 1993. *Managing Change*. Johannesburg: Raven Press.

CULLEN, VALDES ROJAS & ASOCIADOS S.A. 1992. *Plan Argentina 1992*. Buenos Aires: Intera Information Technologies.

CRISTIAN, L.V. 1991. *Soluciones Privadas A Problemas Publicos*. Santiago: Impreso en Editorial Trineo S.A.

DEAN, S.S. & MIDDAUGH II, J.K. 1991. Matching an Organisation's Planning and Control System to its Environment. *Journal of General Management*, Vol. 16, p. 69-84.

D'ARCENI, R.A., MACMILLAN, I.C. & LUCIANI, P. 1990. *Crisis and the Content of Managerial Communications: A Study of the Focus of Attention of Top Managers in Surviving and Failing Firms*. Unpublished Research Report. Hannover: Amos Tuck School of Business Administration, Dartmouth College.

DAVIS, M.A. 1987. *Turnaround — The No-nonsense Guide to Corporate Renewal*. Chicago: Contemporary Books Inc.

DIAMOND, S.C. (Ed). 1985. *Leveraged Buy-outs*. Homewood, Illinois: Dow Jones-Irwin.

DRUCKER, P.F. 1985. *Innovation and Entrepreneurship — Practise and Principles*. London: Heinemann.

DRUCKER, P.F. 1990. *The New Realities*. New York: Harper & Row.

DRUCKER, P.F. 1977. *Management*. New York: Harper's College Press.

DUMAINE, B. 1990. The New Turnaround Champs. *Fortune*, Vol. 122, July 16, p. 24-32.

ECONOMIST GROUP. 1991. *Building Flexible Companies — Strategies and Structures for Fast-moving Markets*. London: Business International Limited (Report No P601).

ECONOMIC COMMISSION FOR LATIN AMERICA AND THE CARIBBEAN, 1992. *Social Equity and Changing Production Patterns: An Integrated Approach*. Santiago: United Nations.

FINANCIAL MAIL. *Special Survey: Top 100 Companies*, May 23, 1986, May 22, 1987, May 20, 1988, May 19, June 1989, June 22, 1990. Johnnesburg.

FINKIN, E.F. 1987. *Successful Corporate Turnarounds — A Guide for Board Members, Financial Managers, Financial Institutions and Other Creditors*. Connecticut: Quorum.

FORTUNE MAGAZINE. *The Search for the Organisation of Tomorrow*. May 18, 1992.

GRINYER, P.H., MAYES, D.G. & MCKIERNAN, P. 1988. *Sharpbenders — The Secrets of Unleashing Corporate Potential*. Oxford: Blackwell.

GUPTA, L.C. 1989. *Corporate Boards and Nominee Directors*. Oxford: Oxford University.

GUY, M.E. 1989. *From Organisational Decline to Organisational Renewal — The Phoenix Syndrome*. New York: Quorum.

HAMBRICK, D.C. & D'AVENI, R.A. 1988. Large Corporate Failures as Downward Spirals. *Administrative Science Quarterly*, Vol. 33, p. 1-23.

HAMEL, G. & PRAHALAD, C.K. 1990. Strategic Intent. *The McKinsey Quarterly*, Spring.

HANDY, C. 1990. *The Age of Unreason*. London: Arrow.

HARRIGAN, K.R. 1985. *Strategic Flexibility — A Management Guide for Changing Times*. Lexington, Massachusetts: Lexington.

HAWKING, S.W. 1988. *A Brief History of Time — From the Big Bang to Black Holes*. London: Bantam Books.

HEENAN, D.A. 1989. The Downside of Downsizing. *The Journal of Business Strategy*, November/December, p. 18-23. Wharton.

HENKOFF, R. 1990. Cost Cutting — How to Do It Right. *Fortune*, April 9, p. 26-33.

HICKMAN, C.R. & SILVA, M.A. 1986. *Creating Excellence*. New York: New American Library.

HIRSCH, S.K. & KUMMEROW, J.M. 1990. *Introduction to Type in Organizations* (2/e). Palo Alto, CA.: Consulting Psychologists Press, Inc.

ITAMI, H. & ROEHL, T.W. 1987. *Mobilizing Invisible Assets*. Boston: Harvard University Press.

KHARBANDA, O.P. & STALLWORTHY, E.A. 1987. *Company Rescue: How to Manage a Company Turn-around*. London: Heinemann.

KIMBERLEY, J.R. & QUINN, R.E. 1984. *Managing Organisational Transitions*. Homewood, Illinois: Irwin.

KIRKPATRICK, D.L. 1987. *How to Manage Change Effectively — Approaches, Methods and Case Examples*. San Francisco: Jossey-Bass.

KOLBE, K. 1993. *Kolbe Team Success Program Leader's Guide*. Phoenix, Arizona: KolbeConcepts Inc.

KOLBE, K. 1990. *The Conative Connection: Uncovering the Link Between Who You Are and How You Perform*. Reading, Mass.: Addison-Wesley.

KOOPMAN, A., NASSER, M.E., NEL, J. 1989. *The Corporate Crusaders*. Johannesburg: Lexicon Publishers.

LAMBERT, L. 1991. Barlows Makes the Market Wonder if Biggest is Still Best. *Business Day*, September 9, p. 6.

LEVITT, T. 1988. The Innovating Organisation. *Harvard Business Review*, January-February, p. 7.

LORSCH, J.W. & MACIVER, E. 1989. *Pawns or Potentates — The Reality of America's Corporate Boards*. Boston, Massachusetts: Harvard University Press.

MACMILLAN, I.C. 1988. Controlling Competitive Dynamics by Taking Strategic Initiative. *Journal of Business Strategy*, Vol. 2, No. 4.

MACMILLAN, I.C. 1984. Preemptive Strategies. *Journal of Business Strategy*, Vol. 4, No. 2.

MACMILLAN, I.C. 1983. Corporate Ideology and Strategic Delegation. *Journal of Business Strategy*, Vol. 4, No. 1.

MACMILLAN, I.C., HAMBRICK, D.C. & DAY, D.L. 1982. The Product Portfolio and Profitability — A PMS-based Analysis of Industrial-product Businesses. *Academy of Management Journal*, Vol. 25, 1/04.

MACMILLAN, I.C. & JONES, P.E. 1984. Designing Organisations to Compete. *Journal of Business Strategy*, Vol. 4, No. 4.

MARTEL, L. 1986. *Mastering Change — The Key to Business Success*. London: Collins.

MEXICAN AGENDA. 1992. *Mexico: The Path Towards Modernity*. Mexico City: Direcion de Publicaciones.

MILES, R.H. & CAMERON, K.S. 1982. *Coffin Nails and Corporate Strategies*. Englewood Cliffs, New Jersey: Prentice-Hall Inc.

MILLS, G. 1985. *On the Board*. London: Allen and Unwin.

INSTITUTE FOR SOCIAL DEVELOPMENT. 1992. *The Montfleur Scenarios: South Africa, 1992-2002*. Cape Town: University of the Western Cape.

NASAR, S. 1988. America's Competitive Revival. *Fortune*, Jan 4, p. 36-43.

NASSER ET AL. 1984. *Project Free Enterprise. Phase 1: Wealth Creation in South Africa*. Pretoria: School for Business Leadership, University of South Africa.

NASSER ET AL. 1986. *Project Free Enterprise. Phase 2: Wealth Creation in South Africa*. Pretoria: School for Business Leadership, University of South Africa.

NASSER ET AL. 1989. *Project Free Enterprise. Phase 3: Wealth Creation in South Africa*. Pretoria: School for Business Leadership, University of South Africa.

NEDCOR-OLD MUTUAL SCENARIOS. 1992. *South Africa — Prospects for Successful Transition*. Cape Town: Juta & Co. Limited.

OHMAE, K. 1990. *The Borderless World — Power and Strategy in the Inter-linked Economy*. London: Harper/Collins.

OHMAE, K. 1983. *The Mind of the Strategist — Business Planning for Competitive Advantage*. London: Penguin Books.

PASCALE, R.T. & ATHOS, A.G. 1982. *The Art of Japanese Management — Applications for American Executives*. New York: Warner Books.

PASCALE, R.T. 1991. *Managing on the Edge — How Successful Companies Use Conflict to Stay Ahead*. New York: Penguin Books.

PETERS, T. 1987. *Thriving on Chaos — Handbook for a Management Revolution*. New York: Knopf.

PETERS, T. & WATERMAN, R.H. 1983. *In Search of Excellence*. New York: Harper and Row.

PORTA, H. 1992. *The Political and Economic Transformation of Argentina*. Speech to Finance Week Breakfast. Johannesburg, April 29.

PORTER, M.E. 1980. *Competitive Strategy — Techniques for Analyzing Industries and Competitors*. New York: MacMillan.

PORTER, M.E. 1980. *Competitive Advantage — Creating and Sustaining Superior Performance*. New York: MacMillan.

QUICKEL, S.W. 1990. Welch on Welch — CEO of the Year. *Financial World*, Vol. 159, April 3, p. 62-68.

SANLAM. 1992. *Platform for Growth*. Pretoria: HSRC (Research Report).

SILVER, A.D. 1988. *When the Bottom Drops — How Any Business Can Survive and Thrive in the Coming Hard Times*. Rocklin, California: Prima.

SIMONS, R. 1987. *Implementing Strategy — Configurations in Management Control Systems*. Unpublished Research Report. Boston, Massachusetts: Harvard Graduate School of Business Administration.

SLATTER, S. 1984. *Corporate Recovery — A Guide to Turnaround Management*. London: Penguin Books.

STALK, G. (Jr) & HOUT, T.M. 1990. *Competing Against Time — How Time-based Competition is Reshaping Global Markets*. New York: MacMillan.

STEWART, J. 1984. *Managing a Successful Business Turnaround*. New York: American Management Associates.

STEWART, T.A. 1991. GE Keeps Those Ideas Coming. *Fortune*, Vol. 124, August 12, p. 18-25.

SUNTER, C. 1992. *The New Century*. Cape Town: Human & Rosseau.

SUNTER, C. 1987. *The World and South Africa in the 1990s*. Cape Town: Human & Rosseau.

TICHY, N. & CHARAN, R. 1989. Speed, Simplicity and Self-confidence — An Interview with Jack Welch. *Harvard Business Review*, September-October, p. 112-120.

TOMASKO, R.M. 1990. *Downsizing — Reshaping the Corporation for the Future*. New York: American Management Association.

TUCKER, B. & SCOTT, B. 1992. *South Africa: Prospects for Transition*. Cape Town: Juta & Co. Limited.

VIVIER, F.J. & MURPHY, J.J. 1991. *Corporate Dynamics: The Mechanics of Organisational Motion During Strategic Turnaround*. Unpublished paper to the International Strategic Society Management Conference. London.

VON KEYSERLINCK, C. 1991. Clive Weil Puts Wheels Back on Limping Game. *Business Times*, May 26, p. 4.

WALKER, J. 1991. Added Value Brings Kudos for Kanhym. *Business Times*, October 20, p. 2.

WOODBURN, T. 1991. Incestuous Corporate Boards Need More Outside Directors. *Business Day*, September 16.